D1364497

365 Pocket™ Prayers for Graduates

Guidance and Wisdom for Each New Day

Tyndale House Publishers, Inc., Carol Stream, Illinois

Visit Tyndale online at www.tyndale.com.

TYNDALE, Tyndale's quill logo, and *LeatherLike* are registered trademarks of Tyndale House Publishers, Inc. *365 Pocket* is a trademark of Tyndale House Publishers, Inc.

365 Pocket Prayers for Graduates: Guidance and Wisdom for Each New Day

Managing editors: Ronald A. Beers and Amy E. Mason

Contributing writers: V. Gilbert Beers, Rebecca J. Beers, Brian R. Coffey, Jonathan Farrar, Jeffrey Frasier, Jonathan Gray, Sean A. Harrison, Sandy Hull, Rhonda K. O'Brien, Douglas J. Rumford, Linda Taylor

Designed by Erik M. Peterson

Edited by Karin Buursma

ISBN 978-1-4143-7542-7

Printed in China

19 18 17 16 15 14 13
8   7   6   5   4   3   2

INTRODUCTION

If you've just graduated, congratulations! You're beginning a new stage of your life when many opportunities may be open to you. We hope this book of prayers will be helpful to you as you navigate the changes ahead.

Prayer is simply talking with God. As people of faith, we can come to him anytime, approach him anywhere, and pray about anything. God loves our honest, heartfelt prayers, and he cares deeply about the details of our lives. As we come before him with praise or petition, we demonstrate that we trust him and long to draw near to him.

Perhaps your faith is relatively new and you're not yet comfortable praying. This book is for you. The prayers we've developed can be claimed as your own conversations with God. As you pray through each topic and day, we hope you will become more comfortable talking with God and will even begin to form your own prayers to him.

Perhaps you've been a believer for years but need a little inspiration in your prayer life. This book is for you, too. We all have times when we repeat the same prayers over and over. Because this book includes a year's worth of unique prayers that cover a broad range of topics, it can help rejuvenate your dialogue with God.

Thank God that we don't have to be spiritually mature or "on fire" to have a meaningful prayer life! Wherever you are in your spiritual journey, God delights when you draw near to him. We hope this little book will help you do so.

You will find 365 prayers, arranged by days and topics. You can pray through each day of the year consecutively if you wish. Alternatively, look in the index for a topic that will help you pray through an urgent need or give words to something you may be experiencing. Every few days you will also find prayers called *Prayerful Moments*. These are shorter prayers for days when time is limited or for when you need a quick word with God.

As you enter into a new prayer, take it slow. Spend some time thinking about what you're saying to God, and try to personalize each prayer for your own life. Making each written prayer your own honest praise or petition will make it more meaningful.

In your conversations with God, take some time to listen. Reading God's Word as a part of your prayer time gives the Lord an opportunity to speak to you, too. You won't want to miss what he has to say! We've included a Scripture verse at the end of each prayer to help you ponder what God might be communicating to you.

Thank you for joining us on this quest for a deeper prayer life. It is our hope that by the end of this book, you will be inspired in your conversations with God and—most important—feel closer to him than ever before. It is often in these special times of prayer that God does his powerful work in our hearts. So don't give up; stick with it. As his Word says to us, "Let us come boldly to the throne of our gracious God. There we will receive his mercy, and we will find grace to help us when we need it most" (Hebrews 4:16).

The privilege of prayer is that it ushers us straight into the presence of our loving God. And Scripture promises us that he won't disappoint! With that in mind, it's time to begin.

☼ A prayer about NEW BEGINNINGS
When I'm nervous about change

LORD,

I'm at a great time in my life for a new beginning. I want a chance to wipe the slate clean and start over, a chance to do something different, a chance to escape from past patterns or hurts. It's exciting to think about taking on new challenges, yet I'm also nervous. The changes ahead will take me away from what's familiar and comfortable. What if I don't succeed? What if I don't like my new circumstances? Help me, Lord, to realize that I can't avoid change. It's just a part of life. Show me the best way to deal with it when it comes. Help me to see it not as a threat but as an opportunity. May I look at each day as a chance to get to know you better and start over with a new attitude. Teach me to trust you with my future.

I am certain that God, who began the good work within you, will continue his work until it is finally finished on the day when Christ Jesus returns. PHILIPPIANS 1:6

☼ A prayer about SEEKING GOD
When I am trying to find God

HEAVENLY FATHER,

I talk to my closest friends almost every day. We go out and do things together, we reminisce about fond memories, or we just enjoy being in the same room. I wouldn't expect to stay close to a friend if I never spent time with him or her. So why do I expect to feel close to you when I don't take time for you? Forgive me. Teach me that my relationship with you takes effort. Prompt me to talk to you every day. I want to be open and honest with you, just as I would be with a close friend. I'd like to tell you about my concerns, think about the future, and remember ways you've helped me in the past. Remind me to listen to you as well, and to think about what you're doing in my life and around the world. Help me commit to reading your Word daily so that I'll be better able to hear your voice and follow your guidance. I want to always remember that you are with me all day, every day. Thank you that you are always available and that I can talk to you about anything, anytime! I'm grateful that when I seek you, I will find you.

My heart has heard you say, "Come and talk with me." And my heart responds, "LORD, I am coming." PSALM 27:8

☼ A prayer about SUCCESS
When I am jealous of others' success

LORD GOD,

Sometimes I get jealous of people who are successful as the world defines it. Maybe they have more possessions than I do, they receive more scholarships or awards, or they are smarter or better liked. But help me to put this jealousy aside and remember that you don't say this kind of achievement is necessarily wrong—in fact, a lot of it is good. At the same time, you tell me to let you set the ultimate measure of success. Help me to put the most energy into pursuing the things *you* think are most important: loving you and those around me, having a godly character, serving you. My earthly achievements and material belongings have no eternal value and will stay here when I die, but your kind of success lasts forever. May I choose wisely which goals I will pursue.

Jesus replied, "'You must love the LORD your God with all your heart, all your soul, and all your mind.' This is the first and greatest commandment. A second is equally important: 'Love your neighbor as yourself.'" MATTHEW 22:37-39

☼ A prayer about RESPECTING OTHERS
When I want to show respect to those in authority

HEAVENLY FATHER,

Many people in my life lead me in some way—my parents, my teachers, my pastor, my boss. I appreciate them, but sometimes I get frustrated with them or think they should do things differently. Even so, I know you want me to treat them with respect. Teach me how to communicate that respect with my words and actions. You call me to encourage them, pray for them, and support them. Keep me from gossiping about them or criticizing them unfairly. If we have a conflict, please give me the courage and wisdom to deal with it privately and graciously. Thank you for the leaders you have put in my life. May I learn from them and please you by the way I treat them.

Dear brothers and sisters, honor those who are your leaders in the Lord's work. They work hard among you and give you spiritual guidance. Show them great respect and wholehearted love because of their work.
I THESSALONIANS 5:12-13

DAY 5

☼ **A prayer about THOUGHTS**
   When I wonder if my thoughts really matter

LORD JESUS,

Sometimes I try to convince myself that it doesn't really matter what I think, as long as I do and say the right things. If I'm outwardly kind to someone, how does it hurt that I'm inwardly making fun of her? But I know that doesn't line up with your Word. You tell me that my thoughts show me the condition of my heart. If I don't catch them in time, sinful thoughts will eventually result in sinful actions. That's because if I think about something long enough, my heart will start trying to convince me that what I want to do is really okay. Please help me to guard my heart and my thoughts, Lord. I know I can't always trust my emotions to tell me what is right because they are skewed by my human nature. I need to trust in your Word because it comes from your heart, which is good and perfect and holy. Please control my heart and my mind. May my thoughts honor you—and may those right thoughts lead to right actions.

Guard your heart above all else, for it determines the course of your life. PROVERBS 4:23

☼ A prayer about PEACE
When I need more of God's peace

LORD JESUS,

How much I need your peace! Teach me that it comes from knowing that nothing can separate me from your love. No matter what happens in my life, you will be with me, and you promise me eternity in heaven. May my confidence in those promises give me the inner peace that comes from you.

[Jesus said,] "I am leaving you with a gift—peace of mind and heart. And the peace I give is a gift the world cannot give. So don't be troubled or afraid." JOHN 14:27

DAY 7 *Prayerful Moment*

☼ A prayer about CHOICES
When I wonder if I've made the right choices

LORD,

When I'm facing a decision, why is it often so difficult to know which is the right choice? Teach me to look to your Word for wisdom and also to seek counsel from wise believers. I know that sometimes there's more than one good answer to a problem. But when there's one choice that's morally right, please confirm it deep in my heart. Give me ears to hear your voice and courage to act on the right choice once I know what it is.

If you need wisdom, ask our generous God, and he will give it to you. He will not rebuke you for asking. JAMES 1:5

DAY 8

☼ A prayer about CONSCIENCE
When I wonder how to keep my conscience active

LORD,

You've given me a conscience to help me know if I'm doing the right thing. I'm grateful for it, but sometimes I have to admit that I tune it out. Forgive me for ignoring its warnings. I know that if I don't obey my conscience, it will become harder and harder for me to hear it. I also know that my conscience won't work properly in isolation. It needs you! Teach me to stay close to you by spending time in your Word. Train me to make an effort to understand myself and my own tendencies toward right and wrong. If I know the areas where I'm most likely to slip into sin, I can guard against them more vigilantly. Keep my conscience from becoming dull and inactive, Lord. I never want to find myself unmoved by evil or uncaring toward injustice. Use my conscience to provide a strong inner sense and a voice of accountability, guiding me to do what is right. I want to be in sync with you. I want to stand before you with a clear conscience.

I always try to maintain a clear conscience before God and all people. ACTS 24:16

☀ **A prayer about FELLOWSHIP**
When I am thankful for relationships with other Christians

LOVING GOD,

Friendship is a wonderful gift, and friendship among believers is even more wonderful. When I experience fellowship with other believers, you promise to be in our midst! Thank you that the church can bring together people who may be very different but who share a common perspective on life. I'm grateful for all the believers around me who encourage me as I walk with you. Help me to pursue genuine relationships within my church so that I have a safe place to share honestly, to be strengthened in the face of temptation and persecution, and to discern godly wisdom when I'm dealing with problems. Show me how to give in relationships as well as to receive. May my fellowship with other believers increase my faith and make me more excited about serving you.

Let us think of ways to motivate one another to acts of love and good works. And let us not neglect our meeting together, as some people do, but encourage one another, especially now that the day of his return is drawing near.
HEBREWS 10:24-25

DAY 10

☼ A prayer about RESPONSIBILITY
When I'm tempted to blame others for my mistakes

HEAVENLY FATHER,

It's so easy to blame others when something goes wrong. If I'm embarrassed about my mistake, I might try to shift some of the blame to another person or some unforeseen circumstance. Why is it so hard to say, "I was wrong"? It really comes down to my pride. I want to appear smart and competent, and I don't want to be associated with mistakes! I don't want to be blamed for what I've done, and I don't want to suffer any consequences. Yet I know I am responsible for my own actions. Please give me the courage to admit when I have made a mistake, without making excuses. Teach me to do whatever I can to fix my error and learn from it so that it won't happen again. As I do, may I be more motivated to do what is right next time. I pray that my trustworthiness will win the respect of others so they will see that you are with me.

Pay careful attention to your own work, for then you will get the satisfaction of a job well done, and you won't need to compare yourself to anyone else. For we are each responsible for our own conduct. GALATIANS 6:4-5

DAY 11

☀ **A prayer about SATISFACTION**
   When I feel dissatisfied

LORD GOD,

When I feel dissatisfied, I must look at how I'm trying to meet my deepest needs. Am I trying to satisfy my soul hunger with the real, good food of you and your Word? Or am I eating the spiritual equivalent of junk food? When I eat food that's not good for me, I get shaky, I can't think straight, and my body doesn't function very well. Show me that the same principle is true on a spiritual level. If I try to satisfy my longings only with fun, pleasure, and sin, I'll just end up empty and craving more. Teach me, Lord, that I need a steady diet of good food for my soul. Let me feed my hunger with your Word and quench my thirst by spending time with you, so that your Holy Spirit can fill me with all the things I need to be a strong and mature believer. You created me to be in relationship with you, so only you can satisfy my deepest cravings. May I always turn to you to find lasting satisfaction.

Let them praise the LORD for his great love and for the wonderful things he has done for them. For he satisfies the thirsty and fills the hungry with good things.
PSALM 107:8-9

☼ **A prayer about COMMUNICATION**
When I need to listen to God

LORD,

When I talk to you, I consider that I'm praying—and I am. But too often I forget that a conversation needs to go both ways. Talking without listening is a monologue, and prayer is supposed to be a dialogue. Forgive me for not paying attention to your words. As I pray, help me to remember that the goal of prayer is to build my relationship with you. You have so much to teach me, and only when I listen can you show me your wisdom and share your resources. Show me how to be quiet before you. As I meditate on you and your Word, let me be ready to hear you speak to my mind and heart. Teach me how to distinguish between my own thoughts and your voice.

Come, let us worship and bow down. Let us kneel before the LORD our maker, for he is our God. We are the people he watches over, the flock under his care. If only you would listen to his voice today! PSALM 95:6-7

☀ **A prayer about MY BEST**
  When I want to give my best to God

LOVING GOD,

I love you. You have adopted me into your family and called me your child! I want to show my gratitude by giving you my best. Teach me to put you first and to give you the best of my time, my money, and my efforts. You are first in my life, and I want my actions to reflect that. May I follow you wholeheartedly.

Honor the LORD with your wealth and with the best part of everything you produce. PROVERBS 3:9

DAY 14 *Prayerful Moment*

☀ **A prayer about COMMITMENT**
  When I wonder what it means to be committed to God

HEAVENLY FATHER,

I know that being committed to you involves both my mind and my will. I've decided to follow you, and now my actions need to provide evidence of that decision. Teach me that commitment brings my thoughts, attitudes, words, and actions together into a common purpose. It means giving my whole self to you while leaving other things behind. That's a sacrifice, but with your help, it's one I'm ready to make.

[Jesus said,] "If you do not carry your own cross and follow me, you cannot be my disciple. But don't begin until you count the cost." LUKE 14:27-28

DAY 15

☼ **A prayer about SERVING**
When I want to follow Jesus' example of serving others

LORD JESUS,

You gave an amazing example of serving others when you were here on earth. You are God—yet you came down to earth in human form, you took on the tasks of a servant when you washed your disciples' feet, and you helped the lowest of the low who came to you for healing. And you did it all with unmistakable compassion, even when the people you were helping could never hope to repay you. Thank you for your example. Please teach me to serve by listening and responding to the needs of those around me. Let me never consider any task degrading or beneath me, but let me be willing to serve in humility. Help me to remember that in your Kingdom, those who seek to be first will be last, but those who are willing to be last will be first. May I be willing to serve others without thinking about what I might gain. Then I will have a heart like yours.

You must have the same attitude that Christ Jesus had. Though he was God, he did not think of equality with God as something to cling to. Instead, he gave up his divine privileges; he took the humble position of a slave and was born as a human being. When he appeared in human form, he humbled himself in obedience to God and died a criminal's death on a cross. PHILIPPIANS 2:5-8

DAY 16

☀ A prayer about VICTORY
When I want to experience daily victories

LORD,

Let me live each day in the victory that comes through Christ. I know your final victory over sin and death is certain; now help me to apply that victory to the daily issues and temptations of my life. Teach me to obey you in the little things—what I say, what I look at, how I react to others, what I think about, how truthful I am. Then I will experience the joy and victory you intend for me right now! Show me that obeying you, even though it requires self-discipline, will steady my heart in times of pain, confusion, loneliness, or distraction. Then when problems and temptations arise, I will already have the habit of focusing on you and trusting you for help. Thank you for giving me victory over sin—both now and in the future.

I have discovered this principle of life—that when I want to do what is right, I inevitably do what is wrong. I love God's law with all my heart. But there is another power within me that is at war with my mind. This power makes me a slave to the sin that is still within me. Oh, what a miserable person I am! Who will free me from this life that is dominated by sin and death? Thank God! The answer is in Jesus Christ our Lord. ROMANS 7:21-25

☼ A prayer about BEING TIRED
When I need strength

LORD GOD,

I am weary—physically weary, but also discouraged, sad, and tired of working so hard for so long. I turn to you for renewed strength. O Lord, refresh my heart as I come to you in praise. Refresh my soul as I come to you in prayer. Refresh my mind as I come to you in meditation and my body as I come to you in solitude. When I draw near to you in thankfulness, please renew my perspective. Encourage me with the knowledge that you are present and you are working, even when I can't see how. You have the power to give new strength that is beyond anything I can understand. Please strengthen me today.

He gives power to the weak and strength to the powerless. Even youths will become weak and tired, and young men will fall in exhaustion. But those who trust in the LORD will find new strength. They will soar high on wings like eagles. They will run and not grow weary. They will walk and not faint. ISAIAH 40:29-31

DAY 18

☼ **A prayer about SPIRITUAL GIFTS**
   When I want to discover my spiritual gifts

FATHER,

Thank you for creating each person on earth with special talents and abilities. Help me to find a way to use mine for your glory, whether it's just as a hobby or eventually in my full-time job. I have to admit that sometimes I think about serving you as an unpleasant duty, but the truth is, I can serve by doing something I enjoy! Help me, Lord, to discover my gifts—not just my talents, but the spiritual gifts you have given me. Maybe it's teaching, helping others, encouraging others, or giving generously. Thank you that I can never use up these gifts. Instead, the more I use them, the more they will be developed and the more effective I will be in serving you.

God has given each of you a gift from his great variety of spiritual gifts. Use them well to serve one another. Do you have the gift of speaking? Then speak as though God himself were speaking through you. Do you have the gift of helping others? Do it with all the strength and energy that God supplies. Then everything you do will bring glory to God through Jesus Christ. All glory and power to him forever and ever! Amen. 1 PETER 4:10-11

DAY 19

☼ **A prayer about FREEDOM**
When I wonder what true freedom is

LORD GOD,

You created all people with the freedom to love and obey you and do what is right—or to disobey you and do what is wrong. Without this freedom, we would never genuinely love you. Sometimes when I am hurting, I wish you had created people so we could make only good choices. What if Adam and Eve hadn't even been able to eat the fruit from the tree you told them to avoid? But then we would be robots, not humans, and we wouldn't ever experience the joy that can come from knowing you. Thank you for providing a way to the ultimate freedom—freedom from sin and death. I am no longer a slave to sin. I am free to love you with my whole heart!

Sin is no longer your master, for you no longer live under the requirements of the law. Instead, you live under the freedom of God's grace. ROMANS 6:14

☼ A prayer about WHAT LASTS
When I am relying on the Bible

HEAVENLY FATHER,

In the fast-changing society I live in, clothes and movies and music become out-of-date so quickly. Sometimes I wonder if anything lasts forever. Yet I know that your Word is constant. The truths and advice in it apply to all people, in all cultures, at all times. Thank you that I can count on the Bible. When I face change, teach me to turn to your Word to maintain my perspective. I know you will give me a rock-solid foundation for my life.

[Jesus said,] "Heaven and earth will disappear, but my words will never disappear." MARK 13:31

DAY 21 *Prayerful Moment*

☼ A prayer about COMPETITION
When I feel overly competitive

LORD,

I have to admit I find satisfaction in doing things better than other people. Yet I know competing against others simply to beat them is not the point. You have called me to work hard and do my best. If I do that, I am following you, whether I win or lose. Remind me that if beating others is my sole goal, I'll only be honoring myself. If doing my best is my goal, I'll be honoring you—the one who created me.

Work willingly at whatever you do, as though you were working for the Lord rather than for people. COLOSSIANS 3:23

☼ A prayer about BALANCE
When I need to maintain balance in my life

LORD JESUS,

Sometimes I think you will be most pleased with me if I keep myself busy all the time with service to you. Yet when I read about your life on earth, I see that you modeled a life of balance between being with others and being alone, between doing and reflecting, between working toward a goal and meditating on God's Word. You worked hard to help others, but then you took time to be renewed spiritually. And that helped you to remain open to God's direction instead of being affected by the circumstances around you. Help me, Lord Jesus, to keep the right pace. May I not move so quickly that I miss your call nor so slowly that I miss the opportunities you send my way. Teach me that I am not responsible for everything, and please give me the wisdom to recognize those things you are calling me to do.

One day soon afterward Jesus went up on a mountain to pray, and he prayed to God all night. At daybreak he called together all of his disciples and chose twelve of them to be apostles. LUKE 6:12-13

☼ A prayer about SIN
When I wonder if my little sins matter

LORD,

When I'm trying to do a big thing for you, does it matter if I sin in the little things? I know it does, but it's so tempting to tell a white lie or cut corners because it will help me reach my end goal that much faster. Please give me the self-discipline to keep myself on the right path. I know that all sin is repugnant to you, no matter whether it's big or small. You care more about my integrity than about the big goal I'm trying to attain. I need your help so that I don't get desensitized to sin. Keep my conscience active so that I don't turn a blind eye to my own wrongdoing. I want to please you not just by what I do, but by how I do it.

Do not let sin control the way you live; do not give in to sinful desires. Do not let any part of your body become an instrument of evil to serve sin. Instead, give yourselves completely to God, for you were dead, but now you have new life. So use your whole body as an instrument to do what is right for the glory of God. ROMANS 6:12-13

DAY 24

⚙ **A prayer about SELF-CONTROL**
When I wonder why self-control is important

FATHER,

I know that the boundaries you give me are put in place so that life will make sense. Without rules, a sporting event would become chaos. People could get hurt, and the game wouldn't keep moving toward a specific goal. I can just imagine a soccer game where half the players decide to use their hands to catch the ball! When I wonder why I need self-control, help me to remember that staying within the boundaries gives me purpose and direction. When I lose control, I'll often have to deal with consequences. That's just the way the world works. Teach me to see boundaries not as negative things that limit my freedom, but as useful things that keep life moving toward the ultimate victory you promise.

Supplement your faith with a generous provision of moral excellence, and moral excellence with knowledge, and knowledge with self-control, and self-control with patient endurance, and patient endurance with godliness, and godliness with brotherly affection, and brotherly affection with love for everyone. The more you grow like this, the more productive and useful you will be in your knowledge of our Lord Jesus Christ. 2 PETER 1:5-8

DAY 25

⚙ A prayer about HOPE
When I need help to persevere

HEAVENLY FATHER,

When life is difficult, I hold on to the hope that someday it will be better. That may come true on earth, but it
will certainly come true someday in heaven. After all, you
offer the ultimate hope: forgiveness from sins and eternal
life with you! Thank you for giving me eternal hope even
at the darkest points of my life. It gives me the strength
I need to persevere, fixing my eyes on the goal ahead. I
know that someday I will live with you, and there will be
no more sorrow, pain, or suffering. May this wonderful
expectation of eternity help me endure the discomforts of
my life today.

*All praise to God, the Father of our Lord Jesus Christ. It is
by his great mercy that we have been born again, because
God raised Jesus Christ from the dead. Now we live with
great expectation, and we have a priceless inheritance—
an inheritance that is kept in heaven for you, pure and
undefiled, beyond the reach of change and decay. And
through your faith, God is protecting you by his power until
you receive this salvation, which is ready to be revealed on
the last day for all to see.* 1 PETER 1:3-5

DAY 26

☀ **A prayer about CONSEQUENCES**
When I am experiencing the consequences of my actions

LORD,

How often I wish I could press a rewind button on my life. When I do something I later regret, I desperately want to go back and erase it. If only I had the chance to do it again, the right way! If only it had never happened. Yet I know that because of the way the world works, most often I will have to deal with the consequences of my actions. You could make my problems disappear, but you choose not to because you want me to learn and grow from my mistakes. I want that too, Lord! May these difficulties in my life not be wasted. Give me eyes to see clearly the wrong choices I made, the will to make them right, and the endurance to deal with the consequences. As I go through this difficult situation, impress on my heart that you are with me always. You love me and want what is best for me. May I learn the lessons you have for me, so that I don't have to repeat my mistakes.

I am waiting for you, O LORD. You must answer for me, O Lord my God. . . . I am on the verge of collapse, facing constant pain. But I confess my sins; I am deeply sorry for what I have done. PSALM 38:15, 17-18

✦ **A prayer about GRACE**
When I am thankful for God's grace

LORD,
I am amazed by your gift of grace. Even though I deserve death because of my sins, you have saved me. You have forgiven me—my sins no longer count against me! Even more, you have promised me eternal life with you one day. My heart is full of gratitude.

The wages of sin is death, but the free gift of God is eternal life through Christ Jesus our Lord. ROMANS 6:23

DAY 28 *Prayerful Moment*

✦ **A prayer about PATIENCE**
When I need patience

MERCIFUL GOD,
Today I am filled with impatience. So many obstacles are in the way of what I want to accomplish, and I'm getting more frustrated every minute. Yet I know that each person I think is in my way has an individual agenda. Please forgive my arrogance in thinking that my goals are more important than anyone else's. I pray for patience and the flexibility to accept that my goals for today may need to change.

We also pray that you will be strengthened with all his glorious power so you will have all the endurance and patience you need. COLOSSIANS 1:11

DAY 29

☼ A prayer about GOSSIP
When I need to change the way I talk about others

LORD JESUS,

Sometimes when I'm talking with my friends about another person, I'm just having fun and I don't realize right away that what I'm doing is gossiping. But then I remember how awful it feels when others talk about me behind my back. I know that gossip is divisive and hurtful. It can separate friends, reveal other people's secrets, and cause a lot of pain. When I gossip about others, I'm judging them based on rumors and opinions—not the facts—and they don't even have a chance to defend themselves. Forgive me, Lord. Help me to become more aware of what I'm saying. Train me to make sure that my words are always true. Teach me to think about how I can build others up, not tear them down. Give me the courage to stop gossip when it begins among my friends. Help me to change the subject or say something kind about the person we're talking about. May my words reflect your love and allow your grace to break through to those around me.

The Scriptures say, "If you want to enjoy life and see many happy days, keep your tongue from speaking evil and your lips from telling lies." I PETER 3:10

DAY 30

☼ **A prayer about GOD'S CALL**
When I want to answer God's call on my life

LORD,

I want to contribute to something significant. I know you created me for a purpose, and I want to discover it. Help me to listen to your call. I know you don't always call people to dramatic, life-changing adventures like being a missionary to the Sudan or starting an orphanage in India. Sometimes you do, but your call for me might be a simple task that's already right in front of me. Maybe it's working in the church nursery, caring for a sick friend, sending a note of appreciation to a professor, volunteering at a homeless shelter, or tutoring a child who needs help with schoolwork. You have given me special gifts and abilities, and I want to use them for you. I know that when I do, I'll be answering your call. And at the same time, I'll be preparing for whatever you have for me in the years ahead. Thank you that when you call me to do something, you promise to equip me with the desire, vision, support, and resources—everything I need to carry it out.

Now may the God of peace—who brought up from the dead our Lord Jesus, the great Shepherd of the sheep, and ratified an eternal covenant with his blood—may he equip you with all you need for doing his will. May he produce in you, through the power of Jesus Christ, every good thing that is pleasing to him. HEBREWS 13:20-21

DAY 31

☀ **A prayer about SPIRITUAL DISCIPLINE**
   When I want to become spiritually mature

LORD,

I want my faith to grow. I want to learn more about you and love you more deeply. I know that spiritual disciplines like Bible study, prayer, fasting, and meditating on Scripture will help me reach these goals. Please help me develop the self-discipline to use them. Remind me that I should never do these things to impress you. You have given me salvation, and there's nothing I can do to earn more of your favor. But when I spend time in spiritual disciplines, you can impress more of yourself on me. As I quietly spend time in your presence and as I read your Word and understand your character better, may I become more like you—and may I also have a positive impact on those around me. Show me how to use my time purposefully and keep my eyes on my goal.

Don't you realize that in a race everyone runs, but only one person gets the prize? So run to win! All athletes are disciplined in their training. They do it to win a prize that will fade away, but we do it for an eternal prize. So I run with purpose in every step. I am not just shadowboxing. I discipline my body like an athlete, training it to do what it should. Otherwise, I fear that after preaching to others I myself might be disqualified. I CORINTHIANS 9:24-27

DAY 32

☼ A prayer about GUIDANCE
When I wish God would show me his plan for my life

ETERNAL GOD,

When I look ahead to my future, sometimes I wish I could know exactly what you have planned for me! Wouldn't it be simpler if I was aware of everything that was going to happen? But I guess then I wouldn't really need to trust you. If I really knew too much about my future, I might be afraid of some hard times ahead or overconfident about my accomplishments. I might stop relying on your wisdom and try to do it all myself. Teach me to have confidence that where I've been, where I am now, and where I'm headed are all part of your plan. Help me to trust your directions, even when I can't see the final destination. I need your guidance, Lord. You don't illuminate the whole journey ahead of me, but you do light up just enough of the path ahead to show me where to take the next few steps. Give me patience as I wait to see what is ahead. Help me to trust that you are revealing as much as I need right now. Thank you for loving me and having my best interests in mind. I trust you.

The LORD is good and does what is right; he shows the proper path to those who go astray. He leads the humble in doing right, teaching them his way. The LORD leads with unfailing love and faithfulness all who keep his covenant and obey his demands. PSALM 25:8-10

DAY 33

☀ **A prayer about RELATIONSHIPS**
*When I wonder what my relationships can teach me
about intimacy with God*

LORD,

I am learning more and more about how to relate to other people, whether it's my family, coworkers, fellow students, or friends. I need your wisdom to understand how you have designed relationships to work. Help me to realize that what I learn about relating to others will help me in my relationship with you. Teach me how to share my heart and thoughts and dreams with someone else. Show me how to want the best for others, to forgive them when they hurt me, and to love them even when they fail. When I do those things, I will be imitating you. I will understand more about the way you love me—and the way I can love you. May I remember that the two greatest commandments are to love you and to love my neighbor. Please open my heart to love more fully.

Jesus replied, "The most important commandment is this: 'Listen, O Israel! The LORD our God is the one and only LORD. And you must love the LORD your God with all your heart, all your soul, all your mind, and all your strength.' The second is equally important: 'Love your neighbor as yourself.' No other commandment is greater than these." MARK 12:29-31

☼ A prayer about HARD-HEARTEDNESS
When my heart is hard

HEAVENLY FATHER,

Why is it difficult for me to give my life to you, even after all you have done for me? Why is it easier for me to react in anger than to forgive? My heart is so hard, Lord. I need you to soften it. I don't want to be stubborn and unyielding. I want my heart to be tender toward you. Transform my heart. May it become one that longs for you.

I will give you a new heart, and I will put a new spirit in you. I will take out your stony, stubborn heart and give you a tender, responsive heart. EZEKIEL 36:26

DAY 35 *Prayerful Moment*

☼ A prayer about THANKFULNESS
When I want to express my gratitude to God

GRACIOUS GOD,

When I want to have a grateful heart, teach me that being thankful for the blessing I've received is only the first step. The next part is being grateful *to you* for the blessing. Then my gratitude will be long-lasting because it will be connected with my trust in your love and care for me. Thank you, Lord, for your faithful love.

Give thanks to the LORD, for he is good! His faithful love endures forever. I CHRONICLES 16:34

DAY 36

☼ **A prayer about BOREDOM**
When I'm feeling bored

HEAVENLY FATHER,

Sometimes I feel so weary. It happens when I've been doing the same thing over and over, when I'm doing work that has no apparent purpose, or when I've been doing nothing for too long. When I feel bored, I know I've lost my passion and my sense of purpose. Help me to recognize this and work against it. I know the best cure for boredom is to find something significant to do—and I know that you have something significant for me. May my eyes be open to the plans you have for my life. May that purpose energize me and guide me as I look for ways to serve you. Then I'll have something to look forward to each day, and I'll also feel your pleasure. When I'm contributing something to your Kingdom, how can I ever be bored?

Let's not get tired of doing what is good. At just the right time we will reap a harvest of blessing if we don't give up.
GALATIANS 6:9

DAY 37

☼ **A prayer about ANGER**
When I don't understand why I get so angry

LORD GOD,
You know the ins and outs of my anger. I get angry when
my pride is hurt or when I don't get my way. When someone rejects me or ignores me, my anger flares as a defense
mechanism to protect my ego. I also get angry when
someone confronts me about something I've done wrong,
because I don't want anyone else to know my failings. But
I know anger is not the right response in these situations.
When anger begins to well up inside me, keep me from
sinning in the way I act and speak. Instead, teach me to
stop and ask myself some questions. Am I really offended?
Is this just about my pride? Am I reacting in humility or
out of revenge? Prompt me to confess my pride and selfish
anger. I know that receiving your forgiveness and pursuing
reconciliation will help melt my anger away.

Sensible people control their temper; they earn respect by
overlooking wrongs. PROVERBS 19:11

DAY 38

☼ A prayer about INSECURITY
When I wonder what I have to offer

LORD,

When I'm in a competitive environment, surrounded by others my age who are trying to succeed at the same things, it's easy for me to start feeling insecure. Am I smart enough? Can I really make it? How can I possibly be significant among all these other people? In those moments I hold on to the promise that you made me in your image. You value me highly. You don't make mistakes; you created me deliberately. You have given me a purpose and the gifts and abilities I need to fulfill that purpose. Teach me to use those abilities for you. May my insecurities never keep me from serving you. Instead, may I find the place where my gifts fit with the needs I see around me. When I find that spot, I pray that my insecurities would melt away so that I can serve you wholeheartedly, without reservation.

You have not received a spirit that makes you fearful slaves. Instead, you received God's Spirit when he adopted you as his own children. Now we call him, "Abba, Father." For his Spirit joins with our spirit to affirm that we are God's children. ROMANS 8:15-16

☼ A prayer about RELEVANCE
When I wonder if the Bible can speak to me

LORD,

I'm staking my life on you as you're revealed in the Bible, so at times I confess I wonder if Scripture is really still relevant. Yet I know that your Word has stood the test of time. Many of the events recorded in it have been confirmed by archaeologists who aren't even believers. I also know that you will not let your words to us disappear from the earth. You have preserved Scripture so that it can guide all believers. Help me to fully trust the Bible's wisdom for my life. Teach me that it is a living document—the words have not changed, but the content is applicable to all generations, cultures, and social classes. May I understand that the Bible first and foremost gives me a picture of who you are, what you have promised, and how I can follow you. It is the cornerstone of my faith. Thank you, Lord, for the wonderful gift of the Bible.

All Scripture is inspired by God and is useful to teach us what is true and to make us realize what is wrong in our lives. It corrects us when we are wrong and teaches us to do what is right. God uses it to prepare and equip his people to do every good work. 2 TIMOTHY 3:16-17

☀ **A prayer about ACCEPTANCE**
   When I'm struggling to accept others

FATHER,

You accept me unconditionally, and I am so grateful. Knowing the love you have for me draws me into a relationship with you. Yet you love me too much to let me stay the same. You challenge me to grow and change. As I look at those around me, help me first to accept them for who they are before I try to influence them. It's easy to accept the people I think are the best or most godly, but that's not what acceptance is all about. Move in my heart, Lord, to give me love for all those around me—even those the world says are unacceptable, like the poor, the homeless, the elderly, and the disabled. Break through my fears, inhibitions, and stereotypes so that I may share your unconditional love with others and, in doing so, bring out the best in them.

May God, who gives this patience and encouragement, help you live in complete harmony with each other, as is fitting for followers of Christ Jesus. Then all of you can join together with one voice, giving praise and glory to God, the Father of our Lord Jesus Christ. Therefore, accept each other just as Christ has accepted you so that God will be given glory.
ROMANS 15:5-7

☼ A prayer about LOVING OTHERS
When I wonder how I can love my neighbor

LORD GOD,

You command me to love my neighbor as myself. That's because you know that my first instinct, because of my sinful nature, is to take care of myself. I know I will never be without sin, Lord, but please teach me to meet the needs of others in the same way I meet my own. Soften my heart that I might learn to genuinely care about others.

If we love each other, God lives in us, and his love is brought to full expression in us. I JOHN 4:12

DAY 42 *Prayerful Moment*

☼ A prayer about CHALLENGES
When I'm facing difficult circumstances

ALMIGHTY GOD,

I'm facing some big challenges right now. Sometimes I'm afraid I won't be able to handle them, but I have faith that you are by my side! You are helping me. Please give me the courage to step out boldly, knowing that you will never leave me.

Commit everything you do to the LORD. Trust him, and he will help you. PSALM 37:5

DAY 43

☼ A prayer about VULNERABILITY
When I need to be vulnerable before God

LOVING LORD,

You know me inside and out—everything I think, say, and do. Sometimes I try to conceal my sin from you out of embarrassment, but that's pointless because you know it already. I can't put up a false front with you; I can't pretend to be something I'm not. Teach me that it's only through full vulnerability that I can find true healing, restoration, renewal, and forgiveness. May I never try to hide from you. Instead, help me to welcome your examination of my heart. Let me answer your call to confess my sin, seek forgiveness, and commit myself to following your ways. Then a great weight will lift off me, because I will know that you have seen me at my worst and still love me. I have nothing to fear and nothing to hide! You know me and you forgive me.

There is no condemnation for those who belong to Christ Jesus. And because you belong to him, the power of the life-giving Spirit has freed you from the power of sin that leads to death. ROMANS 8:1-2

⚙ **A prayer about TEMPTATION**
When I am being tempted

LORD,

I don't like to think about Satan, but the truth is that he is constantly on the attack, trying to tempt me to sin against you. Teach me to stay alert so I can withstand him. Show me how to guard my heart with your Word and stay focused on the path in front of me. May I draw near to you for help, knowing that you will always strengthen me against temptation. Your Word promises that I will not face any temptation that is too great for me to bear! Thank you for that promise. When I do give in to sin, as I know I will sometimes, help me to recognize it, admit it, and correct it. When I am humble before you and receive your forgiveness, sin will lose its hold on me.

Stay alert! Watch out for your great enemy, the devil. He prowls around like a roaring lion, looking for someone to devour. Stand firm against him, and be strong in your faith. 1 PETER 5:8-9

DAY 45

☀ A prayer about JUDGING OTHERS
When I am critical of others

LORD JESUS,

In the Sermon on the Mount, you spoke strongly against judging others. I've been on the receiving end of judging enough to know that it's hurtful and it helps no one. When someone berates me for making a mistake, especially when they don't even tell me how to avoid that mistake again, I shut down and become defensive. I don't want to do that to other people. Help me to remember never to criticize others unless my goal is to help them succeed or improve. If I have constructive feedback, teach me the right way to give it—not harshly or with an intent to humiliate, but gently, privately, and in love. When I'm in a position to give feedback to others, remind me to do it within the context of my relationship with them. May my goal be to help them become the people you created them to be.

Do not judge others, and you will not be judged. For you will be treated as you treat others. The standard you use in judging is the standard by which you will be judged. And why worry about a speck in your friend's eye when you have a log in your own? MATTHEW 7:1-3

DAY 46

☀ A prayer about FEELING ASHAMED
When I'm afraid to share my faith

LORD,

There are people all around me who don't know you. They have never experienced your wonderful love and forgiveness, and they don't understand grace. I see their need, but I have a hard time saying anything to them because I'm afraid I'll be ridiculed. I need courage and perspective, Father. Help me to remember that you don't ask me to go out on a street corner and shout the Good News. Rather, you ask me to be prepared to explain to others why I live the way I do. Teach me to treat others with kindness, that they might see my loving actions and wonder what motivates them. May I never be ashamed of sharing your love with others. Let me know, deep in my heart, that speaking about your mercy and kindness is the kindest, most loving thing I could ever do.

You must worship Christ as Lord of your life. And if someone asks about your Christian hope, always be ready to explain it. But do this in a gentle and respectful way. Keep your conscience clear. I PETER 3:15-16

☼ A prayer about FOCUSING ON JESUS
When I need to keep my eyes on Christ

LORD JESUS,

You are my example. You are the one who goes before me, clearing the path so I can follow behind you. You are the author of my faith! Teach me always to keep my eyes fixed on you. When I'm looking at you, I can never lose my way. You will keep me on the right path. You will bring me ever closer to you. You will help me run the race of faith to the best of my ability, teaching me to get rid of the sin and distractions that hold me back. You inspire me to follow you with joy and perseverance. Thank you, Lord Jesus. I want to do my best for you.

Therefore, since we are surrounded by such a huge crowd of witnesses to the life of faith, let us strip off every weight that slows us down, especially the sin that so easily trips us up. And let us run with endurance the race God has set before us. We do this by keeping our eyes on Jesus, the champion who initiates and perfects our faith. HEBREWS 12:1-2

☼ **A prayer about TRUST**
When I wonder if I can fully trust God

LORD,

Today I need reassurance that I can really trust you. Will you really do what you say you will do? When I doubt, remind me that you are the one who created truth. Truth is the essence of who you are. You cannot lie or go back on a promise. Impress upon my heart that what you promise will always come true. You are trustworthy.

Let us hold tightly without wavering to the hope we affirm, for God can be trusted to keep his promise. HEBREWS 10:23

DAY 49 *Prayerful Moment*

☼ **A prayer about TIME WITH GOD**
When I need to be still before God

LORD JESUS,

In my busy life, I need to be deliberate about taking time with you. Even you, when you were on earth, needed to take time away from ministry and seek rest and reflection. Teach me that finding time to be quiet and meditate on your Word will help me recognize your voice when you speak to me. Help me to find the right balance between working and resting, spending time with people and having quiet time for restoration.

[The Lord says,] "Only in returning to me and resting in me will you be saved. In quietness and confidence is your strength." ISAIAH 30:15

⚙ **A prayer about EXCELLENCE**
When I want to strive for God's standard of excellence

LORD JESUS,

You set the standard for excellence. No scientist or machine can ever duplicate the marvelous complexity of the human body. No artist can paint a picture that rivals one of your sunsets. You do all things well! You want me to pursue excellence, too, because that shows that I care about doing things right and about helping others to the best of my ability. Teach me to do my best in everything I do, whether it's studying, my job, sports, volunteering at church, or just interacting with my family. When I pursue excellence, I'm imitating your character—and so giving others a glimpse of your character. Help me to model myself after you. I'll never be perfect in this life, but as I work toward that goal and become more and more like you, I want to model excellence to those around me.

Work willingly at whatever you do, as though you were working for the Lord rather than for people. Remember that the Lord will give you an inheritance as your reward, and that the Master you are serving is Christ. COLOSSIANS 3:23-24

DAY 51

☼ **A prayer about PRAYER**
   When I wonder if my prayers will be answered

GOD,

When my prayers aren't answered the way I think they should be, I sometimes begin to wonder if you heard them at all. When I start to think that way, help me to picture myself as a child and you as my parent. If you said yes to all my requests, what would happen? I would end up spoiled and probably hurt, because I would receive some things I asked for that really weren't very good for me. Help me to believe that you always answer my prayers according to what you know is best for me. Thank you for loving me enough to say no sometimes. Teach me to pray continually, even if I'm not getting the answer I would like. Give me wisdom to discern when an answer of no might be pointing me in a different direction. Instead of sulking when I don't get what I want, may I trust that you are always working for my good and the good of your Kingdom. That is enough for me.

I love the LORD because he hears my voice and my prayer for mercy. PSALM 116:1

☼ **A prayer about KINDNESS**
When I want to experience God's kindness

LOVING GOD,

Open my eyes to your abundant kindness, which I know is evident all around me. You show your kindness by loving me unconditionally, even when I don't deserve it. You are patient and forgiving when I've sinned. You invite me into an eternal relationship with you. You give me time to turn from my sins and choose your way of life. You bless me in this life and in the life to come. And you meet my needs! You provide for me physically, and you send spiritual refreshment to care for my soul. O Lord, I am overwhelmed by the kindness you have showered on me. May I respond with love and gratitude.

The LORD is merciful and compassionate, slow to get angry and filled with unfailing love. The LORD is good to everyone. He showers compassion on all his creation. All of your works will thank you, LORD, and your faithful followers will praise you. . . . The LORD is righteous in everything he does; he is filled with kindness. PSALM 145:8-10, 17

DAY 53

☼ **A prayer about BROKENNESS**
  When I am at the end of myself

LORD JESUS,

I have nothing to offer right now. I feel so broken. I'm overwhelmed by my circumstances and my sin, and there's absolutely nothing I can do to make things better. I need you, Lord! I prided myself on being self-sufficient, but my pride has come crashing down. Now I see how much I depend on you. Only you can help me out of the mess I'm in. Thank you for caring for me, for being willing to help me, for comforting me in my weakness. You are sufficient for me, Lord. May I always remember that, and as I do, may I share your comfort with others. I know that you can use even this experience to minister to others and to help me grow.

All praise to God, the Father of our Lord Jesus Christ. God is our merciful Father and the source of all comfort. He comforts us in all our troubles so that we can comfort others. When they are troubled, we will be able to give them the same comfort God has given us. 2 CORINTHIANS 1:3-4

DAY 54

☼ A prayer about THE FUTURE
When I wonder what's ahead for me

LORD,

I'm at a crossroads in my life. There are so many choices ahead of me! I'm considering whether to continue with school and where, what kind of job to look for, where to live, and who to spend my time with. When I'm uncertain, help me to remember that you are with me, guiding me. But you don't have a written script for my life that I have to follow word for word. I don't need to worry whether every little decision I make is following your will for my life. You have a final destination in mind for me, but you give me freedom along the way. Teach me to stay close to you, knowing that you can provide comfort, guidance, and blessings as I try to live according to your principles. Even in the midst of my uncertainties and fears about the future, may I cling to you, knowing that you have good plans for me.

"I know the plans I have for you," says the LORD. "They are plans for good and not for disaster, to give you a future and a hope." JEREMIAH 29:11

☼ **A prayer about TIME WITH GOD**
   When I need renewal in my relationship with God

LORD,

I'm in a rut spiritually. When I feel dry and weak, teach me to come to you. You are the one who can renew me. Help me to connect with you through prayer, Scripture, and just being silent in your presence. Please restore my strength and encourage me. Let this be a refreshing time when I can escape from the busy world and take refuge in you.

I wait quietly before God, for my victory comes from him. . . . O my people, trust in him at all times. Pour out your heart to him, for God is our refuge. PSALM 62:1, 8

DAY 56 *Prayerful Moment*

☼ **A prayer about HEALTH**
   When I wonder what God has to say about my physical health

HEAVENLY FATHER,

I know my spiritual life and my physical health are sometimes intertwined. Maybe following your laws won't take away my headache or fix my broken bone, but if I follow your guidelines for life, I'll avoid some habits and choices that are harmful to my body. Teach me to take care of my body because it is a place where your Holy Spirit dwells.

Give your bodies to God because of all he has done for you. Let them be a living and holy sacrifice—the kind he will find acceptable. This is truly the way to worship him. ROMANS 12:1

DAY 57

☼ **A prayer about LISTENING**
When I need to listen more closely to God

LORD GOD,

You are the source of all wisdom and power, yet you want to communicate with me! What a tragedy it would be to let such an opportunity pass me by. Forgive me for taking your words for granted. I don't want to miss anything you say to me, so I need to train my ears to hear your voice. Teach me to listen closely as I pray and read your Word. I know that you can also speak to me through other things, like the words of a close friend, the instruction of a wise teacher, the beauty of a sunset, or the insightful words of a moving song. Help me to pay attention so that I never miss a lesson from you, the master Teacher. I know that the more I listen to you, the more I will hear you and the more I will understand.

Pay attention to how you hear. To those who listen to my teaching, more understanding will be given. But for those who are not listening, even what they think they understand will be taken away from them. LUKE 8:18

DAY 58

☼ A prayer about OPPORTUNITIES
*When I want to make the most of the opportunities
that come my way*

HEAVENLY FATHER,

When I read in your Word the story of Philip, I'm amazed
by how he took full advantage of an opportunity. Philip
followed your leading, and as a result, a powerful official
from a faraway kingdom believed in you and returned
home with the Good News! The opportunities I have in
front of me may not be this dramatic, but they are still
ordained by you. May I never miss the chance to share
your love with others. Teach me to pay careful attention to
the leading of your Spirit, so that I will make the most of
every opportunity.

*An angel of the Lord said to [Philip], "Go south down
the desert road that runs from Jerusalem to Gaza." So
he started out, and he met the treasurer of Ethiopia, a
eunuch of great authority under the Kandake, the queen
of Ethiopia. The eunuch had gone to Jerusalem to worship, and he was now returning. Seated in his carriage,
he was reading aloud from the book of the prophet Isaiah.
. . . Philip asked, "Do you understand what you are
reading?" The man replied, "How can I, unless someone
instructs me?" And he urged Philip to come up into the
carriage and sit with him.* ACTS 8:26-28, 30-31

DAY 59

☼ A prayer about MOTIVATION
When I need spiritual motivation

HEAVENLY FATHER,

I never want to be a spiritual dropout—someone who has lost the enthusiasm to continue a relationship with you. Yet I know that if I lack depth, there will be no place for the seeds of your Word to grow. Then the hot sun of persecution or problems will cause my excitement to wither. I'll lose my sense of purpose, and my connection with you will just slip away. I don't want that, Lord! Keep me close to you. Deepen my understanding of your character, your Word, and your purposes for this world and my life. Increase my enthusiasm for the tasks in front of me. I want to become rooted in you so that I may thrive under your care. May the seed of your gospel grow deep roots in my heart so that my life may produce a fruitful crop for you.

Listen to the explanation of the parable about the farmer planting seeds: . . . The seed on the rocky soil represents those who hear the message and immediately receive it with joy. But since they don't have deep roots, they don't last long. They fall away as soon as they have problems or are persecuted for believing God's word. MATTHEW 13:18, 20-21

⚜ **A prayer about CREATIVITY**
When I want to express my creativity

CREATOR GOD,

I'm grateful for the many ways you have given me to express my creativity. Whether it's through music, art, writing, dance, or something else—and whether I'm actively participating or enthusiastically observing—you allow me to be a part of your rich artistic nature. It's such a gift. I want to be full of the kind of beauty that spills out in wonderful and meaningful ideas, sounds, words, and movements. Help me to take time to fill up on what is beautiful and true. If I want to express your beauty, I need to be filled with your Spirit and your wisdom. Teach me to get to know you, to soak up what is beautiful, and to think about you and all your creative works in the world around me. As I do that, may creative expression flow out of my life in productive ways.

Fix your thoughts on what is true, and honorable, and right, and pure, and lovely, and admirable. Think about things that are excellent and worthy of praise. Keep putting into practice all you learned and received from me—everything you heard from me and saw me doing. Then the God of peace will be with you. PHILIPPIANS 4:8-9

DAY 61

☀ **A prayer about EMOTIONS**
When I wonder how God can help me control my emotions

LORD,

I'm grateful for my emotions. Without them, life would be pretty bland. What if I could never feel joy, excitement, or sympathy? I know that having emotions is a part of being made in your image, because the Bible shows that you experience the full range of emotions, too, from love to anger. I know emotions are a gift, but sometimes mine get out of control. I want my emotions to reflect your character, because then I'll be able to love and serve people in healthy ways. But sometimes they reflect my own sinful nature, and I end up hurting other people because I'm so focused on following my feelings. Teach me, Lord, to understand my emotions and direct them in ways that are productive, not destructive. Help me to remember that it's not wrong to have intense emotions—after all, you do. But may those intense emotions lead me away from sin and toward you.

Clothe yourself with the presence of the Lord Jesus Christ. And don't let yourself think about ways to indulge your evil desires. ROMANS 13:14

DAY 62 *Prayerful Moment*

☼ A prayer about COURAGE
When I am afraid

ALMIGHTY LORD,

I am so afraid, and I feel so small. Yet when I remember that you are with me, my heart begins to take courage. I don't need to be strong to face my problems; you are with me and you offer me your strength. I am weak, but you are powerful. And even more, you care for me in the midst of my troubles. You are my mighty Savior!

The LORD your God is living among you. He is a mighty savior. He will take delight in you with gladness. With his love, he will calm all your fears. ZEPHANIAH 3:17

DAY 63 *Prayerful Moment*

☼ A prayer about DISCERNMENT
When I want to become wise

LORD,

I want to grow in my faith, and I know I need discernment. Teach me that I must discipline my mind and my conscience to distinguish between right and wrong. As I spend more time with you, may I learn to identify temptation before it overwhelms me, recognize truth from lies, and distinguish your voice from all other voices. Then I will be wise.

Tune your ears to wisdom, and concentrate on under-standing. . . . Seek them like hidden treasures. Then you will understand what it means to fear the LORD, and you will gain knowledge of God. PROVERBS 2:2, 4-5

DAY 64

☼ A prayer about HEAVEN
When I wonder how the hope of heaven should affect my life

LORD GOD,

Today I'm thankful for the promise of heaven. I have to admit that it doesn't always feel real to me. There are so many exciting things still ahead of me in this life that I don't often look ahead to heaven. But I know that heaven will be more wonderful than I can imagine. I also know that this life is temporary, while life in heaven will be eternal. You are using my time on earth to prepare me for heaven! May this truth give me purpose in life, perspective on my troubles, and anticipation for the glorious future you have planned for all believers. Teach me to fix my eyes on what will last forever.

Our present troubles are small and won't last very long. Yet they produce for us a glory that vastly outweighs them and will last forever! So we don't look at the troubles we can see now; rather, we fix our gaze on things that cannot be seen. For the things we see now will soon be gone, but the things we cannot see will last forever. 2 CORINTHIANS 4:17-18

DAY 65

⚜ A prayer about PLEASURE
When I wonder what God thinks about pleasure

FATHER,

Some people seem to think it's wrong for Christians to enjoy anything in this world. They frown at a lot of things I think are fun. But that doesn't seem right to me! You are the Creator of all. You are the one who made this world with all its beauties and pleasures. You created a rainbow of colors and a wide variety of food. You gave humans the capacity to make beautiful music, create art, use our bodies for dance and sports, and enjoy friendship. These are good things. Thank you for making them for us to enjoy. Teach me to have the right attitude about pleasure. If I make it my primary goal to get more, I know I'll just end up feeling apathetic and empty. Instead, may I enjoy pleasure as a gift from you. Help me also to remember that the greatest pleasures come from pleasing you and being in your presence. Those pleasures won't fade in a day but will last forever.

You will show me the way of life, granting me the joy of your presence and the pleasures of living with you forever.
PSALM 16:11

⚜ **A prayer about SORROW**
   When I am grieving

MERCIFUL LORD,

I'm experiencing sorrow right now, and I know I'm not alone. Everyone in the world has to deal with grief sometime, whether it's from the loss of a parent, friend, or acquaintance; the loss of innocence through abuse or neglect; or some other difficult situation. Sometimes we know the sorrow is coming and sometimes it comes as a shock, but either way it's an overwhelming feeling. I don't know how to deal with this loss. I'm turning inward, isolating myself from the ones who love me. I'm paralyzed by the sadness and pain, and I feel completely stuck. Will it ever get better? I need your comfort, Lord. I desperately need to see some hope. Help me to cling to the promises in your Word that you are close to me as I grieve. You will not leave me alone in my sorrow. And you promise that one day I will know a world with no more sorrow or pain. I trust you to fulfill that promise.

He will wipe every tear from their eyes, and there will be no more death or sorrow or crying or pain. All these things are gone forever. REVELATION 21:4

DAY 67

☀ A prayer about FLEXIBILITY
When I want to be open to God's plans

LORD,

Do I trust that your timing is perfect? That's what it comes down to when I'm faced with a choice between what I think I should be doing right now and what you seem to be calling me to do. Teach me to be more flexible. I want to have room in my life to change my plans when a special opportunity comes my way—a hurting family member, a friend who is asking questions about faith, an injustice that needs to be righted, a need that must be met. I want to be eager to go where you call me and serve where you place me. Help me, Lord, to hold my plans loosely so that I will be able to grab hold of your plans for me.

The LORD frustrates the plans of the nations and thwarts all their schemes. But the LORD's plans stand firm forever; his intentions can never be shaken. . . . We put our hope in the LORD. He is our help and our shield. In him our hearts rejoice, for we trust in his holy name.
PSALM 33:10-11, 20-21

DAY 68

☼ A prayer about JOY
When I want to experience deep joy

LORD GOD,

I want to know the joy that comes from living in relationship with you. Teach me to pursue the paths to joy: the sense of security that comes from being held by you, the peace of knowing that you accept me for who I am and want me to be with you forever, the quiet confidence of letting you guide me at all times and in all things. Help me to trust that wherever you guide me, it is in my best interests. When I have all these things as my foundation, how can I not experience joy? Then I will know that nothing can shake me. Regardless of my emotional ups and downs, I know that my present and future are secure in your hands. That brings me immense joy.

Let all who take refuge in you rejoice; let them sing joyful praises forever. Spread your protection over them, that all who love your name may be filled with joy. For you bless the godly, O LORD; you surround them with your shield of love. PSALM 5:11-12

DAY 69 *Prayerful Moment*

⚙ **A prayer about EMPTINESS**
When I feel empty inside

LOVING GOD,

When I try to satisfy myself with material things—a new phone, new clothes, a trip to the coffee shop—I feel fulfilled for a while, but then I feel empty again. I know I will only be satisfied when my soul is filled through my relationship with you. As I come to you, please fill me with yourself and your love, help, encouragement, peace, and comfort.

Don't be so concerned about perishable things like food. Spend your energy seeking the eternal life that the Son of Man can give you. JOHN 6:27

DAY 70 *Prayerful Moment*

⚙ **A prayer about PEACE**
When I need to make peace with others

GOD OF PEACE,

You call me to pursue peace, and you bless me when I bring your peace to others. Teach me to live in harmony with those around me. Help me to remember that living in peace doesn't mean that I will never experience conflict. Instead, it means that I can deal with conflict appropriately, filled with confident assurance. Show me how to be a peacemaker wherever I go.

Make every effort to keep yourselves united in the Spirit, binding yourselves together with peace. EPHESIANS 4:3

DAY 71

☼ **A prayer about ACCOUNTABILITY**
When I need to be accountable to God

LORD JESUS,

Sometimes there are dark corners of my life that I'd just as soon keep hidden. I don't want to share them with anyone, even you, because I'm ashamed of what you will find there. Help me to remember that you know all the secrets of my heart anyway. Trying to hide from you never helps me—it only hurts me. Being accountable to you may not be comfortable, but I know it's necessary. Teach me to be honest with you about the struggles I'm facing. Direct me and encourage me as I try to follow the principles for living I find in your Word. Then I know I will be less likely to do something I will later regret. You are my accountability partner, God! May I always understand that you are guiding me to a fuller, more purposeful life.

Search me, O God, and know my heart; test me and know my anxious thoughts. Point out anything in me that offends you, and lead me along the path of everlasting life.
PSALM 139:23-24

☼ A prayer about ENERGY
When I need to approach my tasks with more energy

LORD,

I'm so busy. How can I have more energy to tackle all the tasks in front of me? Help me to remember first of all that in everything I do, I am working for you. That gives my responsibilities a divine purpose and reminds me that you are my audience. If I'm doing things for myself, I don't always take the time or energy to do them well. Instead, I do them partway or sloppily so I can finish quickly. But when I'm working for you, I want to do things well. I want to present you with a finished product that is carefully done to the best of my ability, so that it will honor you. Teach me to do each task as an act of love and service to you. Then I will be infused with energy.

Work with enthusiasm, as though you were working for the Lord rather than for people. Remember that the Lord will reward each one of us for the good we do. EPHESIANS 6:7-8

☼ A prayer about HARD-HEARTEDNESS
When I need to be more responsive to God

HEAVENLY FATHER,

When I read the story of the Prodigal Son, I can relate to the older brother all too well. I'm so concerned about getting what I think is mine that I don't always respond to other people with grace. Punishment and judgment come more easily to me than forgiveness. I don't always trust you to do what is best for me, so I'm always on the lookout for my own interests. How can my heart become open to you? I want to be pliable—ready to be changed by you and ready to be used by you. Soften my heart, Lord. I need your help. May I be moved to joy by the things that bring you joy and moved to sorrow by the things that bring you sorrow. May I be full of love for you.

The older brother was angry. . . . "All these years I've slaved for you and never once refused to do a single thing you told me to. And in all that time you never gave me even one young goat for a feast with my friends. Yet when this son of yours comes back after squandering your money on prosti- tutes, you celebrate by killing the fattened calf!" His father said to him, "Look, dear son, you have always stayed by me, and everything I have is yours. We had to celebrate this happy day. For your brother was dead and has come back to life! He was lost, but now he is found!" LUKE 15:28-32

DAY 74

☼ A prayer about FORGIVENESS
When I need a second chance

LORD GOD,

I am so thankful that you give second chances—and third chances, and fourth chances, and on and on! I read in your Word that when the Israelites turned away from you and worshiped idols, you sent prophets time and time again to call them back. Even after the Israelites were exiled to Babylon, you allowed some to come back and rebuild the wall around Jerusalem. Then you told them that if they humbled themselves, turned away from their sin, and called on you, you would forgive them and restore their land. That's an amazing promise. I've messed up again and again, and I know I need to face the consequences. But you always welcome me back. When I am sincerely sorry for my sins, I can come to you for forgiveness and ask you to help me start over again. You want me to be reconciled to you. I praise you, Lord! May I never take this for granted but always come to you readily, asking for and receiving forgiveness.

If my people who are called by my name will humble themselves and pray and seek my face and turn from their wicked ways, I will hear from heaven and will forgive their sins and restore their land. 2 CHRONICLES 7:14

DAY 75

☼ **A prayer about FRIENDSHIP**
When I want to build friendships that will last

LORD,

Friends are gifts from you, especially those who share a commitment to honor you. Thank you for the example of David and Jonathan, who were close friends even when, by some standards, they should have been enemies. After all, Jonathan was King Saul's son and next in line for the throne, while David had been anointed by God to take the throne after Saul. Yet the two remained friends to the end, even through lots of difficult circumstances. Please help me to be that kind of committed friend—one who is loyal, supportive, and encouraging. When my relationships are tested, may those challenges draw my friends and me together rather than pulling us apart. May we be good influences on each other and draw each other closer to you. Thanks for the gift of friendship.

David . . . met Jonathan, the king's son. There was an immediate bond between them, for Jonathan loved David. From that day on Saul kept David with him and wouldn't let him return home. And Jonathan made a solemn pact with David, because he loved him as he loved himself. Jonathan sealed the pact by taking off his robe and giving it to David, together with his tunic, sword, bow, and belt. 1 SAMUEL 18:1-4

☀ **A prayer about MERCY**
  When I need God's mercy

LORD GOD,
Be merciful to me, a sinner. I know I have made choices that alienate me from you. I have acted selfishly, spoken unkindly, hurt others, been motivated by pride, and turned away from your loving guidance. Yet you extend your mercy to me. You invite me to confess my sin, repent, receive your forgiveness, and enter into fellowship with you. Thank you, Lord.

Let us come boldly to the throne of our gracious God. There we will receive his mercy, and we will find grace to help us when we need it most. HEBREWS 4:16

DAY 77 *Prayerful Moment*

☀ **A prayer about DOING WHAT IS RIGHT**
  When I want to please God with my actions

HEAVENLY FATHER,
When I feel pressured to cut corners or do something less than honest, please help me to stay true to my commitment to do what is right. I want to follow your path for living. Give me the courage to resist pressure and do what is kind, fair, honest, and just—no matter what. I know you will bless me for doing the right thing.

The LORD rewarded me for doing right. He has seen my innocence. To the faithful you show yourself faithful; to those with integrity you show integrity. PSALM 18:24-25

☼ A prayer about HABITS
When I've developed bad habits

LORD,

I want to be in charge of the choices I make and the paths I pursue, but now I realize that when I try to be in control, I end up losing control to other things. Wrong desires have sneaked in and set up a routine of bad habits. Now those bad habits seem to be controlling me! I need your help, Lord. I want to be freed from these sins that bind me, but when I try to get loose just by using more self-control, I get stuck again. Teach me that the only answer is turning over control of my life to you. You are the only one who can transform me from the inside out. You can help me change not only my behavior but also the thoughts and desires that are at the core of the problem. Turn my heart toward you. May I seek your help through prayer and seek support from other believers. I know you can break the chains that hold me. You are the one who can set me free from the control of bad habits.

Those who are dominated by the sinful nature think about sinful things, but those who are controlled by the Holy Spirit think about things that please the Spirit. So letting your sinful nature control your mind leads to death. But letting the Spirit control your mind leads to life and peace. ROMANS 8:5-6

⚙ **A prayer about TIME WITH GOD**
When I need to be strengthened for what's ahead

LORD,

As I take time with you today, may I be still and prepare myself to hear you speak. Teach me to meditate on you and listen for your voice. I want to be ready to hear you speak to my heart and mind so that I will know your will for me and will be ready to do it. Teach me also that you are strengthening me in these moments with you, preparing me for whatever lies ahead. I know I will face temptations and struggles. I pray for the discipline to train myself so that I will have the spiritual wisdom, strength, and commitment to honor you, no matter what comes. Deepen my roots and help me to grow in you. Thank you for the refuge of your presence and your love.

I pray that from his glorious, unlimited resources he will empower you with inner strength through his Spirit. Then Christ will make his home in your hearts as you trust in him. Your roots will grow down into God's love and keep you strong. EPHESIANS 3:16-17

☼ A prayer about BURNOUT
When I need strength to keep going

MY GOOD SHEPHERD,

I am exhausted and stressed, and I don't know how I can keep going. I feel worn out spiritually, emotionally, mentally, and physically. The world is moving so quickly around me that I can't keep up. I know it will help to take care of myself physically by getting good nutrition and enough sleep. But even more important is to be close to you. Let me draw near to you, Lord! I need to experience the quiet rest that comes only from you. I'm tired of trying to be in charge, so please teach me to let you lead me. Help me to focus on your Word and let it minister to me. Reshape my priorities and show me your perspective. Ease my fears and restore my strength. Let me tap into your power, your strength, your protection, and your love. Thank you for loving me no matter what.

The LORD is my shepherd; I have all that I need. He lets me rest in green meadows; he leads me beside peaceful streams. He renews my strength. He guides me along right paths, bringing honor to his name. PSALM 23:1-3

☀ A prayer about INTEGRITY
When I want to be known as a person of integrity

LORD JESUS,

I want to live with integrity, and I know there's no better model to follow than you. I can never be perfect as you are, but I know I can always grow in integrity. Teach me to be faithful in every area of my life, no matter how small. It's only by practicing faithfulness in each little decision that I'll be able to be faithful when the big decisions come. When my honesty is tested, please help me to remember that my actions have consequences. The choices I make every day combine to forge my reputation and develop my character. I want to have a rock-solid character, Lord Jesus, and I know the best thing I can do is emulate you. May my life reflect your compassion, honesty, purity, and wisdom. Then others will see you in me, and I will be a person of integrity.

If you are faithful in little things, you will be faithful in large ones. But if you are dishonest in little things, you won't be honest with greater responsibilities. LUKE 16:10

☼ A prayer about PEACE
When I am fearful

LORD GOD,

This world can be a scary place. Sometimes my imagination runs away with me and I think about all the terrible things that could happen to me or my family. How can I have peace? I need your help, Lord. Teach me that you are always watching over my soul. Your peace will not prevent me from encountering difficulties, but it will prevent me from encountering them alone. By promising me salvation through the gift of your Son, you also promise to give me the final victory over all my troubles. One day all the problems and evil of this world will be gone, yet my soul will still be secure with you. May I hold on to that hope. As it sinks deep into my heart, may I be filled with the peace that is beyond all human comprehension—the peace that comes from knowing you.

I am convinced that nothing can ever separate us from God's love. Neither death nor life, neither angels nor demons, neither our fears for today nor our worries about tomorrow—not even the powers of hell can separate us from God's love. No power in the sky above or in the earth below—indeed, nothing in all creation will ever be able to separate us from the love of God that is revealed in Christ Jesus our Lord. ROMANS 8:38-39

☼ A prayer about OPPORTUNITIES
When I want to take the opportunities God gives me

LORD GOD,

I don't want my life to be defined by opportunities I missed. When I recognize that you're giving me a chance to participate in your purposes, please give me the courage to respond with bold action. I want to take advantage of every opportunity you put in front of me, whether it's for evangelism, serving others, or learning something new. Teach me to make myself available to you.

Make the most of every opportunity in these evil days. Don't act thoughtlessly, but understand what the Lord wants you to do. EPHESIANS 5:16-17

DAY 84 *Prayerful Moment*

☼ A prayer about COMMUNICATION
When I want to recognize God's voice

LORD,

Sometimes I think you are speaking to me. How can I be certain that it's your voice I'm hearing? If I don't know you, how can I recognize your voice? I want to get to know you more and more through your Word and through prayer. Just as a sheep recognizes its shepherd's voice without question, I want to be able to know and respond to your voice right away, without any doubts. Give me ears to hear you, Lord.

[Jesus said,] "My sheep listen to my voice; I know them, and they follow me." JOHN 10:27

☼ A prayer about SIN
When I need to acknowledge my own sin

LORD,

I don't really like the word *sin*. I know people make a lot of bad choices, but to call them sin makes me uncomfortable. It sounds so black-and-white and judgmental. Yet the truth is, from your Word I know that there's an objective standard of right and wrong, established by you. When I violate it, I'm sinning and separating myself from you. Help me to accept this teaching, not to fight against it or deny it. That's as pointless as arguing with a doctor who has just diagnosed a terrible disease and prescribed treatment. Rather than railing against the unpleasant news, I should be thankful that there is a cure. Sin is a disease that can destroy my life if left unchecked, but you have provided a way to deal with it. Teach me always to admit my own faults and acknowledge that I need your help. I have sinned against you, Lord, in word and in deed. You alone can forgive me, cleanse me, and set me on the path to eternal life. Thank you for your wonderful gift of salvation.

If we confess our sins to him, he is faithful and just to forgive us our sins and to cleanse us from all wickedness.
1 JOHN 1:9

☼ A prayer about MEANING
When I wonder how God can bring meaning to my life

FATHER GOD,

When I think about the Christian life as a bunch of rules, it seems boring. But when I realize that following you is all about relationship, not rules, it becomes full and exciting. At great cost to yourself, you saved me from an empty, meaningless life to give me one of great value. You love me, you created me for a specific purpose, and you want to work through me to accomplish your work in the world. There's nothing boring about that. I pray that this knowledge will affect every area of my life. May it change my outlook, infusing it with meaning and purpose as I catch your vision and direction for me. Help me to find my place in this life and in your Kingdom. Through me, pour out your blessings to others.

God paid a ransom to save you from the empty life you inherited from your ancestors. And the ransom he paid was not mere gold or silver. It was the precious blood of Christ, the sinless, spotless Lamb of God. 1 PETER 1:18-19

☀ A prayer about SHARING
   When I want God to multiply my offerings

LORD,

I'm amazed by the story in your Word about the young boy who shared his lunch with Jesus. It was just a small thing compared to the huge need—more than five thousand hungry people—but in Jesus' hands, five loaves and two fish became more than enough. Teach me that sharing benefits others even more than I realize. I may never know how my act of generosity helped someone else, but I can trust that you will use it to the fullest. Help me to share joyfully and freely because you have shared so generously with me. May I give to others as an expression of my love for you. Just like the little boy, I know I'll be amazed by how you can multiply my offerings.

"There's a young boy here with five barley loaves and two fish. But what good is that with this huge crowd?" . . . Then Jesus took the loaves, gave thanks to God, and distributed them to the people. Afterward he did the same with the fish. And they all ate as much as they wanted. JOHN 6:9, 11

DAY 88

☼ A prayer about PERSPECTIVE
When I need to see others through God's eyes

LORD GOD,

I know I jump to conclusions about people. I see a few things about them—their appearance, their level of wealth or success, how much they volunteer, or their demeanor during a few short minutes of conversation—and then assume I can evaluate how close they are to you. Forgive me, Lord. Teach me to see people from your perspective. Remind me that a person's spiritual status has very little to do with externals and everything to do with humbly receiving salvation through faith in Jesus. I'm grateful that you alone know my heart, and that you alone are in control of my eternal destiny. Keep me from judging others; remind me that it's not my job to determine whether any particular person is in or out of your Kingdom. Instead, help me to extend love to all those around me, whether or not they follow you.

Note this: Some who seem least important now will be the greatest then, and some who are the greatest now will be least important then. LUKE 13:30

DAY 89

⚙ **A prayer about AWE**
   When I am in awe of God's power

MY GREAT CREATOR,

Who is like you? You have made everything in the universe, and nothing happens without you knowing. You give life and breath to everything on earth, and each moment of my life is in your hands. When I get even a glimpse of how powerful you are, I am amazed. Yet you have called me your own! I don't have to be afraid of you. I would take cover from the power of a severe storm and run from a crashing wave on the shore, yet being in awe of your power draws me toward you instead of away from you. Teach me to see more of your awesome power at work in my life and in the world around me. As I do, may I be drawn closer to you. Fill me with your powerful Holy Spirit, and give me eyes to see your amazing presence all around me.

I have heard all about you, LORD. I am filled with awe by your amazing works. In this time of our deep need, help us again as you did in years gone by. And in your anger, remember your mercy. HABAKKUK 3:2

☼ A prayer about STRESS
When I have too much to do

LORD,

When I'm feeling stressed, I start to panic. I can't concentrate on what I need to do because I'm so worried about what I might not get done! Please calm my mind and quiet my thoughts. Teach me to bring my worries to you and leave them there. Then help me to focus on one thing at a time, doing each one to the best of my ability. I need your strength and peace.

The LORD gives his people strength. The LORD blesses them with peace. PSALM 29:11

DAY 91 *Prayerful Moment*

☼ A prayer about MY WITNESS
When I wonder how my testimony can help others

LORD GOD,

When I get scared by the word *witness*, help me remember that to witness simply means to tell about something I have experienced. I have had the privilege of experiencing your love and forgiveness, and I want to be willing to share that with others. Teach me always to be ready to tell the story of how I came to know you and love you. May you use my testimony for your glory, to draw others to you.

How beautiful are the feet of messengers who bring good news! ROMANS 10:15

☀ **A prayer about BUSYNESS**
When I need to be still before God

LORD,

When I wake up in the morning, my mind is filled with all the activities I have planned for the day. There are phone calls to make, deadlines to meet, assignments to complete, work to do, and people to see. I could run from morning until night and still not accomplish everything I need to do. Yet in the midst of all this busyness, you call me to be still. Even when I don't think I can afford to give up a minute, you tell me to make time for you. Oh Lord, please help me have the discipline to do this. Quiet my racing mind and calm my anxious thoughts. Clear away the clutter and help me to see clearly what is really important. I cannot come into your presence and leave unchanged. I know that when I am still before you, you will transform my heart and renew my mind. Then I will be equipped to face my busy day, secure in the knowledge that following you is my key priority in life.

Be still, and know that I am God! I will be honored by every nation. I will be honored throughout the world.
PSALM 46:10

⚙ **A prayer about INVITATION**
When I wonder how to respond to Jesus' invitation

LORD JESUS,

You have extended the greatest invitation of all—you have invited me to follow you. But it's just an opportunity until I decide to accept it. What if Peter and Andrew had responded to your call with a polite refusal or by putting you off until later? They wouldn't have become your disciples and would have missed being a crucial part of your ministry. Help me to remember that your invitation demands a decision. I can choose to follow you, or I can stay where I am. Staying where I am might seem easier, but in the long run I will be missing out on so much—a relationship with you, abundant life, and a joyful eternity. Just as Peter and Andrew left their nets to follow you, give me the courage to take action. May I respond to your invitation with a joyful, enthusiastic yes!

Jesus called out to them, "Come, follow me, and I will show you how to fish for people!" And they left their nets at once and followed him. MATTHEW 4:19-20

DAY 94

☀ **A prayer about WARNINGS**
When I sense that God is warning me

LORD GOD,

I encounter warnings all the time. A red light warns me to stop. An ambulance siren warns me to get out of the way. A poison label on a cleaning product warns me not to consume it. When I'm getting close to something dangerous, you give me warnings too—sometimes through your Word and sometimes through my conscience. Teach me not to look at these warnings as intrusions that prevent me from enjoying life, but as blessings that protect me so that I can enjoy life more. Help me to understand that your warnings are designed to shield me from the consequences of foolish actions. Then I won't rebel against you but will trust your direction for my life.

The laws of the LORD are true; each one is fair. They are more desirable than gold, even the finest gold. They are sweeter than honey, even honey dripping from the comb. They are a warning to your servant, a great reward for those who obey them. PSALM 19:9-11

☼ A prayer about SPIRITUAL WARFARE
When I want to prepare myself for spiritual battle

FATHER,

I don't think about it very often, but your Word clearly teaches that humans are involved in a spiritual battle. My faith puts me right in the middle of it. Help me to recognize this, not ignore it or pretend it's not true. Show me how to arm myself so I will not be defeated. You give me the tools I need through your Word, because in it you expose Satan for who he is. As I read Scripture, please shine the light of truth on Satan's lies, teach me how to prepare for his attacks, and give me wisdom to fight his tricks and strategies. You are equipping me to fight this battle, but it's most comforting to know that you will not abandon me. The battle is ultimately in your hands, and you will claim the victory.

Be strong in the Lord and in his mighty power. Put on all of God's armor so that you will be able to stand firm against all strategies of the devil. For we are not fighting against flesh-and-blood enemies, but against evil rulers and authorities of the unseen world, against mighty powers in this dark world, and against evil spirits in the heavenly places. EPHESIANS 6:10-12

☼ A prayer about INFLUENCE
When I want to plant seeds of faith

LORD,

I want my life to count for you. I don't want to go through the motions of the life of faith, doing just enough to get by. I want to have a godly influence on others. Help me to remember that on this side of eternity, I may never see how my life affects others. Even so, I need to be faithful to live in obedience to you. I pray that through my words and actions, I will plant seeds of faith in the lives of those around me. May some of these seeds grow into a saving relationship with you. Teach me that I am not responsible for the outcome; you are the one who makes the seeds grow. My responsibility is to live every day in fellowship with you, growing more like you in character and integrity. May my life then influence others to draw near to you.

After all, who is Apollos? Who is Paul? We are only God's servants through whom you believed the Good News. Each of us did the work the Lord gave us. I planted the seed in your hearts, and Apollos watered it, but it was God who made it grow. It's not important who does the planting, or who does the watering. What's important is that God makes the seed grow. 1 CORINTHIANS 3:5-7

DAY 97 *Prayerful Moment*

☀ **A prayer about MY PAST**
When I need a fresh start

LORD OF THE FUTURE,

No matter what I have experienced in the past, you are ready to give me a new start. Whether I look back and smile at loving memories or cringe at wrong choices that now fill me with regret, you are ready to help me move forward. You alone can forgive me, heal me, cleanse me of sin and guilt, and help me start anew. Free me, Lord, to live in peace with purpose and joy.

[The Lord says,] "I will forgive their wickedness, and I will never again remember their sins." HEBREWS 8:12

DAY 98 *Prayerful Moment*

☀ **A prayer about WORK**
When I want to find meaning in my work

LORD,

Teach me that work is a gift, not a curse. After all, you created work before the Fall, when you asked Adam to care for the Garden of Eden. Teach me to honor you with my work by striving for excellence, serving others, and seeking purpose and beauty. Show me that, ultimately, I am working for you.

Whatever you do or say, do it as a representative of the Lord Jesus, giving thanks through him to God the Father.
COLOSSIANS 3:17

⚙ A prayer about STRENGTH
When I want my strength to be tempered by love

MIGHTY GOD,

People around me think that following you means being weak. They assume that I trust in you because I can't make my own decisions or handle life on my own. But the truth is, it takes great strength to obey you when I'm tempted to sin, and it takes great courage to serve others through acts of kindness when I don't feel like it. Please build up my strength so that I can handle these situations. But help me always to remember that strength and power are not the same. When I strive for power, I'm trying to exert control. Show me that in your Kingdom, the strongest thing to do is love, no matter what. In fact, your Word says that if I don't love others, I am nothing, no matter how strong or accomplished I am. I pray that as I grow in faith, my life will exemplify power under the control of love.

If I could speak all the languages of earth and of angels, but didn't love others, I would only be a noisy gong or a clanging cymbal. If I had the gift of prophecy, and if I understood all of God's secret plans and possessed all knowledge, and if I had such faith that I could move mountains, but didn't love others, I would be nothing. 1 CORINTHIANS 13:1-2

DAY 100

☼ A prayer about ADDICTION
*When I wonder if God can break the power of
addiction in my life*

FATHER,

I know what an addict really is—a slave, chained to a life
of bondage. I don't want to be enslaved to a habit or a
substance. Whether my addiction is to drugs or alcohol,
pornography, overeating, gaming, or anything else, I want
to be free. Teach me that the worst addiction of all is sin.
It seems attractive when I am tempted, and sometimes I
justify giving in just this once, thinking I have it all under
control. But then I realize that I'm stuck in a habit I can't
stop. I don't have the self-control to fix this, Lord, but I
know you can help me. You are more powerful than any
problem I face. Break the power of my addictions and help
me to give you control of my life. Release me from my
slavery, transform me, and make me free.

*You belong to God, my dear children. You have already won
a victory . . . because the Spirit who lives in you is greater
than the spirit who lives in the world.* I JOHN 4:4

☼ A prayer about FUN
When I feel as if there's no room for fun in the Christian life

LORD JESUS,

A lot of the people around me seem to think that following you takes all the fun out of life. They think being a Christian means being serious all the time, working hard all the time, and losing a sense of humor. To be honest, sometimes I feel that way too! But then I remember that you are the creator of joy. You made this world with so many good things for us to do and see and experience. It's true that some things the world considers fun go against your rules, and those I should always avoid. But help me to understand that the best kinds of fun—laughing with friends, experiencing the joy that comes from loving relationships, celebrating life milestones with family—honor you because they reflect your character. In this world I will experience times of sorrow, but I'm so thankful that I'll also experience times of great joy and laughter.

For everything there is a season, a time for every activity under heaven. . . . A time to cry and a time to laugh. A time to grieve and a time to dance. ECCLESIASTES 3:1, 4

☼ A prayer about DISAPPROVAL
When I don't like the actions of those around me

LORD JESUS,

Sometimes I just don't approve of what those around me are doing. Whether it's my classmates, my coworkers, or my family members, I see people making choices that aren't very smart and that go against your guidelines for life. How do I keep my disapproval from affecting my attitude toward these people? Maybe the best way is to remember what you did while you were on earth. I picture you hanging around with "good," churchgoing people, but that's far from the truth. When I read the Gospels, I'm reminded that you found the very people who appeared to be the furthest from you and ministered to their needs. Help me to follow your example. Give me discernment to look beyond people's behavior to the reasons behind it. Show me how to love them wholeheartedly. Teach me, Lord Jesus, to reach out and serve others in love.

"Zacchaeus!" [Jesus] said. "Quick, come down! I must be a guest in your home today." Zacchaeus quickly climbed down and took Jesus to his house in great excitement and joy. But the people were displeased. "He has gone to be the guest of a notorious sinner," they grumbled. . . . Jesus responded, ". . . The Son of Man came to seek and save those who are lost." LUKE 19:5-7, 9-10

☀ **A prayer about GOD'S WILL**
When I wonder what God's will is for my life

LORD,

This is an exciting point in my life, but it can also be scary. So much is changing, so many possibilities are in front of me, so many things are still unknown. I wish I knew exactly what you want me to do with my life. Yet I know that in your Word you have already revealed a lot of your will for all believers. Teach me to take these guidelines to heart—instructions like worshiping only you, loving both my friends and my enemies, using my spiritual gifts, staying sexually pure, refraining from gossip, being generous, not taking your name in vain, reading your Word regularly, not letting money control me, letting the Holy Spirit control my life, and trying to know you better and better. The list goes on! I pray that obedience to your ways will shape my life in all the years ahead, no matter what specific paths I may take.

Oh, that we might know the LORD! Let us press on to know him. He will respond to us as surely as the arrival of dawn or the coming of rains in early spring. HOSEA 6:3

DAY 104 *Prayerful Moment*

☼ A prayer about ACCEPTANCE
When I'm thankful for the way God accepts me

LORD GOD,

I know that accepting others is the key to good relationships. Not doing so leaves me isolated and lonely, but when I can accept others and feel accepted by them, I can develop friendships. Thank you for accepting me—even though at times I've hurt you, ignored you, or rejected you. I praise you for loving me unconditionally. Now please help me to extend that unconditional acceptance to others.

[Jesus said,] "Those the Father has given me will come to me, and I will never reject them." JOHN 6:37

DAY 105 *Prayerful Moment*

☼ A prayer about FAITH
When I wonder how faith fits in with what I've been taught

LORD GOD,

Sometimes it seems that my faith and what I was taught in my academic studies have nothing in common. They're two separate spheres in my life. But I know that's the wrong way to think about learning. All knowledge comes from you! You are the source of all wisdom, so why would I think your truths have nothing to do with my education? Give me eyes to see your perfect truth all around me.

Everything was created through him and for him.
COLOSSIANS 1:16

DAY 106

☀ A prayer about EXPERIENCE
When my work feels insignificant

LORD,

Sometimes I wonder if the experience I am getting now is really preparing me for anything worthwhile in the future. Yet I know that you waste nothing; you can use everything to further your purposes. Teach me to do my best wherever I am, trusting that you are using this experience to prepare me for something ahead. After all, your Word tells me about David, whose years as a shepherd didn't seem to do anything to prepare him to be a king. Yet because of his background, he eventually ruled not as a tyrant but as the shepherd-king Israel needed. Thank you that no matter how insignificant I feel my current work is, you can use it to shape me and bring you glory. May I make the most of where you have put me today. Show me how to serve you right here, trusting you to bring significance to the insignificant.

He chose his servant David, calling him from the sheep pens. He took David from tending the ewes and lambs and made him the shepherd of Jacob's descendants—God's own people, Israel. He cared for them with a true heart and led them with skillful hands. PSALM 78:70-72

✲ A prayer about INVOLVEMENT
When I want to reach out to others

LOVING GOD,

It's easy to be a bystander. It takes a lot more energy to become involved, especially in a situation that might be messy or complicated. Sometimes I'm not even sure what to do. So when I see someone in need or observe something I could do to help, I'm often tempted to turn a blind eye and pretend I don't notice. But I know that is not your way. You are love, and you have called all believers to a life of love. Forgive me, Lord. Help me to remember that I am to be compassionate and active, ready and willing to go the extra mile. I want to experience more of you and your love as I get involved in the lives of others.

[Jesus said,] "I am giving you a new commandment: Love each other. Just as I have loved you, you should love each other. Your love for one another will prove to the world that you are my disciples." JOHN 13:34-35

☼ A prayer about HURTS
When others have hurt me

LORD,

I know that when you forgive, you wipe away the past and forget it. You call me to practice this kind of forgiveness too, but it can be so difficult when someone has hurt me deeply. I need your help, Lord. Create in me the desire to forgive. I know that forgiving others will remove bitterness from my soul and begin the healing process. Help me to remember that my sin hurts you deeply too, yet you are willing to forgive me and restore my relationship with you. I want to follow your example. I don't want to live with bitterness. Thank you for caring about my hurts. Now teach me that it's only by forgiving those who have hurt me that I can be free to experience your comfort and peace of mind. Thank you for your incredible forgiveness.

Since God chose you to be the holy people he loves, you must clothe yourselves with tenderhearted mercy, kindness, humility, gentleness, and patience. Make allowance for each other's faults, and forgive anyone who offends you. Remember, the Lord forgave you, so you must forgive others.
COLOSSIANS 3:12-13

☀ **A prayer about THE HOLY SPIRIT**
When I need to remember that the Holy Spirit dwells in me

LORD JESUS,

On the Day of Pentecost, when the Holy Spirit came upon the believers, you were fulfilling a promise you had made to the disciples. And when they experienced that amazing miracle, it must have been another confirmation that you were who you said you were and that you would do what you had promised. You had not left them alone, but you were equipping them for whatever was ahead. I may not see the Holy Spirit working in my life as dramatically as the disciples did that first day, but I know he is dwelling within me. You have not left me alone. You are equipping me for whatever is ahead. You will do what you have promised—both now and in eternity.

When you believed in Christ, he identified you as his own by giving you the Holy Spirit, whom he promised long ago. The Spirit is God's guarantee that he will give us the inheritance he promised and that he has purchased us to be his own people. He did this so we would praise and glorify him. EPHESIANS 1:13-14

☼ **A prayer about HONESTY**
When I wonder why I should be honest

HEAVENLY FATHER,

I'm honest most of the time about most things—but sometimes I bend the truth about little things. Is that really so bad? I guess deep down I know the answer. Honesty matters to you because it reveals my character. If I twist the truth or cheat in little things, I'm just making it harder for myself to be honest when bigger stakes come along. Help me to remember that it doesn't matter if anyone sees me. You always do. Teach me that my true character is revealed when I think no one is looking. Forgive me for the times when I'm less than honest, Lord. I want to live a life of integrity, and I know that total honesty will give me a strong foundation. May my life be governed not by the world's standards of fairness and justice, but by yours.

Who may climb the mountain of the LORD? Who may stand in his holy place? Only those whose hands and hearts are pure, who do not worship idols and never tell lies. They will receive the LORD's blessing and have a right relationship with God their savior. PSALM 24:3-5

DAY 111 *Prayerful Moment*

☼ **A prayer about BUSYNESS**
   When I need rest

LORD,

Too often I think that if I'm busy, I'm being productive, and if I'm resting, I'm being lazy. Yet sometimes I stay busy with things that don't matter, while the most important things in my life are left behind. Show me how to find a balance between working, serving, having fun, and resting. Then I'll be productive in all areas of my life, and my priorities will better align with yours.

Let my soul be at rest again, for the LORD has been good to me.
PSALM 116:7

DAY 112 *Prayerful Moment*

☼ **A prayer about REPENTANCE**
   When I need to repent

MERCIFUL GOD,

I realize that I'm going the wrong way in life. I've been stuck in sin, and I need to get out. I need to come before you in repentance. I don't want to keep repeating this sin; I want to change! Help me to stop what I'm doing. Change the direction of my life, Lord. I am sorry for what I've done, and I need your help to get back on the right path.

Repent of your sins and turn to God, so that your sins may be wiped away. ACTS 3:19

☼ A prayer about ABSOLUTES
When I wonder what I can count on

FATHER,

Sometimes everything seems relative, and I wonder if there are any absolutes in life. How can I know? But then I remember that your Word is my instruction manual. In it, you have given me instructions for living that are true for all times and all people. After all, you are the creator of life! Who else can know absolute principles that explain the best way to live? Teach me that when I don't do things your way, life won't work right and I'll just end up frustrated and disappointed. I don't want to miss out on all that you intend for me to enjoy. May I commit to reading the Bible regularly so I can learn what really works to make life smoother, more enjoyable, and more fulfilling.

All Scripture is inspired by God and is useful to teach us what is true and to make us realize what is wrong in our lives. It corrects us when we are wrong and teaches us to do what is right. God uses it to prepare and equip his people to do every good work. 2 TIMOTHY 3:16-17

☀ A prayer about ANTICIPATION
When I want to anticipate my eternal future

FATHER,

I love the hush that comes in a theater when the house-lights are dimmed and the curtain starts to rise. That's the excitement of anticipation. I want to feel that same excitement when I think about what is ahead of me. You have a purpose for my life; you want to do things in me and through me. Teach me to be still before you so I can be open to your plan. But help me also to look ahead to the most exciting thing of all: the future you have prepared for all believers. You are giving us a priceless inheritance that will never fade away! May I never forget this, and may I continually be filled with joy and anticipation as I consider the glorious things you will do one day.

Now we live with great expectation, and we have a price-less inheritance—an inheritance that is kept in heaven for you, pure and undefiled, beyond the reach of change and decay. And through your faith, God is protecting you by his power until you receive this salvation, which is ready to be revealed on the last day for all to see. So be truly glad. There is wonderful joy ahead, even though you have to endure many trials for a little while. 1 PETER 1:3-6

⚙ **A prayer about FAILURE**
   When I wonder what God considers failure

LORD,

When I think of success, I think about having a good job, living in a nice part of town, or having a lot of friends. I spend some of my time working toward things like that. Yet you say that if I accomplish all these things but do them apart from you, I'm failing. The only way I can be successful in your eyes is to acknowledge my need for you, accept your gift of salvation, and live the way you have called me to live. Help me to choose that way always! I know that you have my best interests in mind. You want to help me make the most of life, both now and forever. You want me to build my life on your solid foundation. No matter what accomplishments I gain in this world, may I also gain the most important one of all: knowing you.

[Jesus said,] "Anyone who listens to my teaching and follows it is wise, like a person who builds a house on solid rock. Though the rain comes in torrents and the floodwaters rise and the winds beat against that house, it won't collapse because it is built on bedrock. But anyone who hears my teaching and doesn't obey it is foolish, like a person who builds a house on sand. When the rains and floods come and the winds beat against that house, it will collapse with a mighty crash." MATTHEW 7:24-27

☀ A prayer about PATIENCE
When it's taking a long time to reach my goals

LORD GOD,

Life doesn't always go exactly the way I want it to, and then I get impatient. I know what I'm trying to accomplish, and I want it now! But focusing on my own agenda and priorities only leads to frustration. Teach me to have a broader perspective on life. If I see it as a winding journey instead of as a straight line between two points, maybe I'll start to realize that what I do along the way may be more important than when I reach my goal. I need to learn not to be in such a hurry all the time. Show me how to be patient when things don't go the right way, trusting that you may have a reason for the delay. Instead of wasting my time in anger over obstacles I can't control, may my eyes be open for ways I can serve others as I wait. Life will have detours from my perspective, but teach me that in your grand plan, if I'm following you I'm always on the right path.

We also pray that you will be strengthened with all his glorious power so you will have all the endurance and patience you need. May you be filled with joy, always thanking the Father. COLOSSIANS 1:11-12

☀ A prayer about PRAYER
When I wonder if God hears my prayers

HEAVENLY FATHER,

I have to admit that at times I wonder if you are paying attention to my prayers. Are they just bouncing off the ceiling? Does it do any good to pray when I don't seem to get answers? But when I think carefully about the questions I'm asking, I realize that they all have to do with how prayer benefits me. Too often I assume that you're not answering when the truth is that you're just not answering exactly the way I expected. Help me to remember that the bigger question about prayer is whether I am paying attention to your response. Sometimes even when things work out just as I'd hoped, I forget to thank you and don't give you the credit. Forgive me, Lord. I know you are loving and good, and that it's in your nature to give good things to your people. Teach me to trust your heart and thank you for your answer, because I can be confident that whatever it is, it's in my best interests.

Devote yourselves to prayer with an alert mind and a thankful heart. COLOSSIANS 4:2

☼ **A prayer about ENTHUSIASM**
When I need fresh motivation to serve God

LORD GOD,

Following you is a serious decision. But at the same time, I find such delight in knowing that you, the God of the universe, love me and have a plan to use me in a powerful way! May I serve you enthusiastically and joyfully. I know my greatest motivation comes not from a sense of duty but from love for you and joy in doing your work.

Restore to me the joy of your salvation, and make me willing to obey you. PSALM 51:12

DAY 119 *Prayerful Moment*

☼ **A prayer about POTENTIAL**
When I want to achieve my potential

LORD,

Thank you for creating me in your image. I know that means I have the potential to reflect all of your wonderful characteristics—such as love, faithfulness, integrity, patience, and wisdom. What an incredible promise! May I allow you to control my life and develop my spiritual potential. Thank you for the Holy Spirit, who lives in my heart, develops your fruit in me, and helps me reflect you.

We are God's masterpiece. He has created us anew in Christ Jesus, so we can do the good things he planned for us long ago. EPHESIANS 2:10

⚙ A prayer about RISKS
When I want to take a risk for God

FATHER,

I feel you calling me to something new. Maybe it's a new job or a different volunteer opportunity. Maybe it's just taking the risk of reaching out to someone who could be a new friend or who needs a hand. Maybe it's something big, like going on a missions trip or working abroad for a year. Help me to be open to what you have for me. I pray for discernment to figure out what it is, and the courage and faith to take a risk to serve you in a new way.

It was by faith that Noah built a large boat to save his family from the flood. . . . It was by faith that Abraham obeyed when God called him to leave home and go to another land that God would give him as his inheritance. He went without knowing where he was going. . . . Abraham was confidently looking forward to a city with eternal foundations, a city designed and built by God. HEBREWS 11:7-8, 10

☀ A prayer about GRATITUDE
When others sacrifice for me

LORD JESUS,

I'm not always sure how to respond when someone makes a sacrifice for me. My parents might sacrifice a higher standard of living to pay for my continuing education, or sacrifice their wants to pay for my needs. My friends might sacrifice their time to be with me or their reputation to defend me. My boss might sacrifice his or her time to help me master a new procedure at work. May I never take these sacrifices for granted, Lord. When I'm so preoccupied with my own needs, it's easy to take what others give without even acknowledging the cost to them. But I want to be a person of gratitude. Teach me to pay attention to what others are doing for me and to take time to thank them wholeheartedly. Thank you for the people in my life who love me enough to help me every day. And thank you most of all for your ultimate sacrifice on the cross, which brought me salvation.

This is real love—not that we loved God, but that he loved us and sent his Son as a sacrifice to take away our sins.
I JOHN 4:10

☀ **A prayer about TESTING**
 When I wonder if God tests my faith

LORD GOD,

Your Word makes it clear that you never tempt people to
sin, and I'm grateful for that. But I know you sometimes
test me. Just as my teachers have tested me to help me
improve my performance, so you sometimes test my faith
to strengthen me and help me accomplish everything you
want me to do. Teach me to respond to these tests not
with frustration or anger, but with a sense of expectancy,
because they mean that you are working in my life. You
love me too much to let me stay just as I am. You are
constantly working to transform me into your image—
into the person I was created to be. You want to purify
me, move me toward spiritual maturity, strengthen my
relationship with you, and increase my influence on those
around me. O Lord, please give me patience and endurance in times of testing. May I trust you fully, knowing
that you have my best interests in mind.

*Dear brothers and sisters, when troubles come your way, con-
sider it an opportunity for great joy. For you know that when
your faith is tested, your endurance has a chance to grow. So
let it grow, for when your endurance is fully developed, you
will be perfect and complete, needing nothing.* JAMES 1:2-4

※ A prayer about STUBBORNNESS
   When I need to break out of my stubbornness

LORD,

My stubbornness sometimes gets me in trouble. I find myself unwilling to budge from whatever position I've already stated, even though I know I may be wrong. I need your help to get over my pride and admit that I may need to change my mind. I don't want my stubbornness to hinder my faith, but I know it does. Teach me that I'm being stubborn when I refuse to believe that you can make a difference in my life, when I let circumstances convince me that you don't care, when I stop praying because I've made up my mind that it doesn't help anyway, or when I refuse to trust you and instead depend on my own strength. Forgive me, Lord, for shutting you out and refusing to acknowledge that you know better than I do. Please help me to be humble, admitting that I don't always know best. Break through my stubbornness and let me experience your love and renewal.

Be careful then, dear brothers and sisters. Make sure that your own hearts are not evil and unbelieving, turning you away from the living God. You must warn each other every day, while it is still "today," so that none of you will be deceived by sin and hardened against God. For if we are faithful to the end, trusting God just as firmly as when we first believed, we will share in all that belongs to Christ. HEBREWS 3:12-14

⚙ **A prayer about ROMANCE**
   When I'm hoping to share my life with someone

LOVING GOD,

You've created me to desire relationships. Without friendships, I feel isolated and lonely. I'm grateful for my friends, but right now I'm longing for something more: a romantic relationship. I want to experience the joy of sharing my life with someone, both the good and the bad. I long to feel the emotional highs of being connected with someone. You created romantic love, Lord, so I know it's a good thing. But is it the right thing for me now? Teach me to be patient, waiting for the right time and the right person. Help me not to rush things but to allow romance to grow out of friendship, shared values and experiences, and the common goal of loving and serving you. I know your timing is perfect. You love me more than any person ever could, and you want what is best for me. I pray that I will trust you for this area of my future.

For everything there is a season, a time for every activity under heaven. . . . A time to cry and a time to laugh. A time to grieve and a time to dance. A time to scatter stones and a time to gather stones. A time to embrace and a time to turn away. ECCLESIASTES 3:1, 4-5

DAY 125 *Prayerful Moment*

☼ A prayer about TIME
When I need help managing my time

LORD,

When I'm so busy I'm not sure how everything will get done, my time with you is usually the first thing that goes out the window. I know that's not the right solution. Teach me, Lord, that the best way to find the time I need is to devote *more* time to you, not less. As I spend time in prayer, I know you will remind me of my priorities. I can't do everything, but you will always provide enough time for what's most important.

Teach us to realize the brevity of life, so that we may grow in wisdom. PSALM 90:12

DAY 126 *Prayerful Moment*

☼ A prayer about LONELINESS
When I feel alone

LORD GOD,

When I feel lonely, help me to remember that you are here with me. You are thinking about me all the time. I am not abandoned! May I never give up on you when I feel alone. Instead, may I use times of isolation to discover your faithfulness and your love.

Those who know your name trust in you, for you, O LORD, do not abandon those who search for you. PSALM 9:10

☀ A prayer about OBEDIENCE
When I wonder why it's so important to obey God

LORD GOD,

Please increase my desire to obey you. When I'm tempted to go against your commands, remind me that they are in place for my own good, to protect me from harm. May I never reject your authority. Teach me that obeying you frees me to enjoy life as you intended, because it keeps me from becoming entangled in harmful situations. I know that obeying you will bring blessing, joy, and peace. Help me to obey out of love and gratitude, not out of fear or duty. The more I obey out of love, the more I will want to obey because I find joy when pleasing you. I trust that you want what is best for me.

Oh, the joys of those who do not follow the advice of the wicked, or stand around with sinners, or join in with mockers. But they delight in the law of the LORD, meditating on it day and night. They are like trees planted along the riverbank, bearing fruit each season. Their leaves never wither, and they prosper in all they do. PSALM 1:1-3

DAY 128

☼ **A prayer about RESPONSIVENESS**
When I want to be in tune with God

HEAVENLY FATHER,

How can I live in harmony with you? I want to become more and more like you. I want to think the way you think and care about the things you care about. I want my life to reflect you and glorify you. But how? I guess it's like a piano being tuned against a standard tuning fork. I know I will be in tune with you when I check myself against the standards of living found in your Word. As you communicate with me through the Bible, I will begin to discern more about who you are and how you are calling me to live. And as I open myself to your Holy Spirit, you will be working in my heart, transforming me into your image. Improve my spiritual hearing, Lord. May my ears always be tuned to your voice, and may I respond readily whenever I hear you calling me to a certain task.

The word of God is alive and powerful. It is sharper than the sharpest two-edged sword, cutting between soul and spirit, between joint and marrow. It exposes our innermost thoughts and desires. HEBREWS 4:12

☼ A prayer about ENDURANCE
When I am tired of the journey

LORD,

Sometimes I feel as if I'm running a marathon. I'm in the middle of a grueling race, I'm exhausted, and I can't see the finish line. I need endurance to complete this journey of life. I know that there are tangible rewards for finishing strong—a reputation others can respect, fellowship with you, a legacy of faith. But the best reward of all is the prize of spending eternity with you. Teach me endurance, Lord. I know that as I run this race, you are right beside me. You will never leave me, and you will never stop working in me. May I have the strength to persevere, to keep doing the right things, to keep following you, to keep on in this life of faith. I know the rewards will be great.

Pursue righteousness and a godly life, along with faith, love, perseverance, and gentleness. Fight the good fight for the true faith. Hold tightly to the eternal life to which God has called you, which you have confessed so well before many witnesses. I TIMOTHY 6:11-12

☼ A prayer about PLANS
When I wonder if it's okay to make plans

LORD GOD,

I'm at a point in my life where I'm making a lot of plans: plans for the next step in my education, plans for the kind of job I'd like to have, plans for where I'd like a relationship to go, plans for where to live. So many things in my life are up in the air, and I'm working hard to figure out which of the many opportunities I should pursue. Yet sometimes I wonder if making plans means that I'm trying to be in control of my life instead of trusting you. Teach me to hold my plans loosely, Lord. I believe that you have given me the wisdom to make good choices about my future, but I know that ultimately you are in charge. Help me to plan wisely, yet be open to the unexpected detours that may come my way. May I be willing to veer from my plans when it becomes clear that you have another path for me. Thank you for caring so deeply about my life.

The LORD will work out his plans for my life—for your faithful love, O LORD, endures forever. PSALM 138:8

☼ A prayer about KNOWLEDGE
When I want to use my knowledge effectively

HEAVENLY FATHER,

I can find updated information everywhere I turn and learn new things every day. Yet having knowledge doesn't make me wise; it's what I do with the information that counts. If I know a lot about the Bible, theology, and the difference between right and wrong but don't apply it, it all goes to waste. I'm no better off than if I'd never learned any of it! Teach me, Lord, to use all my knowledge toward making a positive difference in my life and the lives of those around me. Help me to remember that meaningful knowledge begins with understanding who you are and respecting what you say. May I apply my wisdom in such a way that it will transform me and draw me closer to you.

If you are wise and understand God's ways, prove it by living an honorable life, doing good works with the humility that comes from wisdom. . . . The wisdom from above is first of all pure. It is also peace loving, gentle at all times, and willing to yield to others. It is full of mercy and good deeds. It shows no favoritism and is always sincere. JAMES 3:13, 17

☼ A prayer about GOD'S PROMISES
When I need assurance

GOD OF TRUTH,

You are all-powerful, yet there is one thing you cannot do: you cannot lie. I praise you because everything you have promised will come true. In moments of doubt, teach me to rehearse your promises: you are with me always, you forgive sins, you have offered me the free gift of salvation, you will return one day and bring me to heaven. May these wonderful promises strengthen my faith day by day.

Let us hold tightly without wavering to the hope we affirm, for God can be trusted to keep his promise. HEBREWS 10:23

DAY 133 *Prayerful Moment*

☼ A prayer about SUFFERING
When I want to comfort those who are suffering

FATHER,

Someone close to me is hurting, and I want to help. Please show me how to reach out. Keep me from saying thoughtless things or trying to figure out the reason for this struggle, when the truth is I don't really know. Teach me instead to join in my friend's suffering—to choose to be wounded along with him, to hurt along with her. Help me to share the truth of your presence. May my compassion bring comfort and hope.

Share each other's burdens, and in this way obey the law of Christ. GALATIANS 6:2

☀ A prayer about SELF-CONTROL
When I need self-discipline

LORD,

I am really struggling with self-control. I know what I should do, but all too often I just don't do it. I give in to temptation, blow up in anger, take the easy way out instead of doing the right thing. Please help me to develop more self-control. Just trying harder doesn't work, because it's not just my effort that's lacking but my will. I need your transforming power in my life so I will want to make the right choices. When I need self-discipline, teach me to turn to you, admit my need, and ask you to help me do the right thing. You have told me in your Word that you have given me a spirit of self-discipline, and I cling to that. I know you are faithfully working in my heart. Thank you for helping me.

God has not given us a spirit of fear and timidity, but of power, love, and self-discipline. 2 TIMOTHY 1:7

☀ **A prayer about GOD'S TIMING**
When I am frustrated with waiting

FATHER,

I hate to wait. When I get stuck driving behind a slow car or waiting in a long line, I get edgy. And it's even harder for me to wait for bigger things in life. I get especially frustrated when I have prayed and prayed for what clearly seems like the right thing, but you don't seem to act. I believe you want what is best for me—but I want it now! I feel as if I'm stuck in limbo and can't move forward. Teach me to trust your timing, Lord. I can't see what's up ahead, but you can. You are in control of my life, and you are able to make things happen at just the right time. Help me to wait quietly for you to act, trusting that you will do what is best, when it's best.

I wait quietly before God, for my victory comes from him. He alone is my rock and my salvation, my fortress where I will never be shaken. . . . Let all that I am wait quietly before God, for my hope is in him. PSALM 62:1-2, 5

DAY 136

☼ A prayer about VALUES
   When I want my values to reflect God's

LORD,

It's easy to say that I value my faith above everything else, but how can I know for sure? Teach me that the kind of entertainment I enjoy, the things I think about most, and the way I spend my money can give me a window into what is most important to me. Whatever I consider important, useful, and worthwhile is what I really value. Please help me to see clearly where my values align with yours and where the world's values are shaping me. Soften my heart so that I can be shaped by your priorities. Teach me to love the things you love and pursue the things you pursue. I want others to see through my actions that I love you, and that your love for me has transformed my life. May my commitment to you shine through all I say and do.

Wherever your treasure is, there the desires of your heart will also be. . . . No one can serve two masters. For you will hate one and love the other; you will be devoted to one and despise the other. You cannot serve both God and money. MATTHEW 6:21, 24

☼ A prayer about HOLINESS
When I wonder how I can ever be holy

HOLY LORD,

When I hear people say that Christians should be holy, I feel discouraged. How can I ever be free of sin? It seems like an unattainable goal since you alone are perfect. Yet your Word tells me that holiness is my ultimate goal, and it will be a reality one day when I stand before you in heaven. Teach me that holiness doesn't come from my own striving; I could try harder and harder each day and still not be totally pure when I'm old and wrinkled. You are the one who makes me holy. Only you have the power to cleanse me from sin and let me stand before you as white as snow. Right now I am still fighting with my sinful nature, forgiven yet still turning back to sin time and time again. But you have promised that someday, all that will be behind me. Thank you, Lord, for your complete forgiveness that will allow me one day to stand before you holy and blameless.

You were cleansed; you were made holy; you were made right with God by calling on the name of the Lord Jesus Christ and by the Spirit of our God. I CORINTHIANS 6:11

☀ A prayer about INJUSTICE
When I want to do something about injustice

HEAVENLY FATHER,

I know that people all over the world are being treated unjustly. It happens in countries far away, and it happens right around me. I pray that I will never become blind to it. Your Word is clear that you hate injustice, so I know I need to hate it as well. Teach me never to look away when I see unfairness around me, whether it's people being denied their rights, being cheated, or being accused of things they didn't do. Give me the courage to speak up and be a voice for those who have no voice. When I can change something, help me to act. I know that compared to many people in the world, I'm in a position of privilege. I pray that I will never let that harden my heart toward those who are defenseless. Let me do what is right, motivated by your love for all people, no matter what their status.

Learn to do good. Seek justice. Help the oppressed. Defend the cause of orphans. Fight for the rights of widows.
ISAIAH 1:17

☼ A prayer about VICTORY
When I want to reflect on Christ's victory over sin

LORD JESUS,

Whenever I am discouraged by my sinful nature, help me to remember that you have won the ultimate victory over sin. Because of your great sacrifice, I am no longer a slave to sin! You have freed me. Your death, resurrection, and forgiveness allow me to be completely cleansed. Now, in gratitude, may I pursue you with all my heart.

Thank God! Once you were slaves of sin, but now you wholeheartedly obey this teaching we have given you. ROMANS 6:17

DAY 140 *Prayerful Moment*

☼ A prayer about SOLUTIONS
When I need to find the right solution to a problem

LORD,

I have a big problem, and I'm not sure how to fix it. What's worse is that I created the problem—it came from my own hasty mistake. I'm so tempted to blame someone else for what happened, but help me to realize that would only make my problem bigger. Acknowledging and dealing with my mistakes can be embarrassing, but I know it's the only way to find a solution and regain other people's respect. Please give me humility and wisdom as I deal with this crisis.

Enthusiasm without knowledge is no good; haste makes mistakes. PROVERBS 19:2

DAY 141

✦ A prayer about FAITH
When I wonder how my faith should affect my life

LORD JESUS,
If I really have faith in you, I will trust you with my life.
Faith means far more than just believing in something—
like the way I believe that green is a nice color or that
babies are cute. It means entrusting my life to what I
believe, or rather, to who I believe in. I do trust you, Lord
Jesus. Please grow my faith. I want to be willing to follow your guidelines for living, because I trust that your
will is best for me. I want to be willing even to endure
ridicule and persecution for my faith because I am sure
that you are who you say you are. You are the Creator, the
all-powerful Judge, the Prince of Peace, and the Savior. I
trust that you will keep your promise to grant believers
salvation and eternal life in heaven. Sometimes my faith
seems small, but as I remember your promises and your
character, it will continue to grow.

*Faith is the confidence that what we hope for will actually
happen; it gives us assurance about things we cannot see.*
HEBREWS 11:1

☀ **A prayer about LIFE'S DEMANDS**
When I'm not sure how to cope

MIGHTY GOD,

Right now the demands on me seem impossible. The tasks are too hard, the burdens are too much for me to bear, and my schedule is too full to keep up with. How can I cope? My faith in you is the only thing keeping me going right now. I know you are my greatest source of help. You are almighty God—the God of the impossible. Nothing is too hard for you. When life seems overwhelming, my only choice is to turn to you. I admit that I can't deal with this on my own. I give you control of my life. I know that when I allow you to carry the burden for me, you will give me the strength to continue.

He gives power to the weak and strength to the powerless. Even youths will become weak and tired, and young men will fall in exhaustion. But those who trust in the LORD will find new strength. They will soar high on wings like eagles. They will run and not grow weary. They will walk and not faint. ISAIAH 40:29-31

☼ A prayer about DOUBT
When I wonder if it's okay to question my faith

LORD GOD,

I admit that sometimes I wonder if everything I believe is true. I love you and I stake my life on you, yet I still have doubts once in a while. Is that okay? I'm reassured by the biblical examples of many who doubted—like David, John the Baptist, Peter, and Thomas. You brought them all through their doubts to a stronger, more vibrant faith. May it be the same for me. I know that doubt can be sinful if it leads me away from you into long-term cynicism, skepticism, or hard-heartedness. But that's not what I want. I pray that my honest searching will lead me even closer to you and strengthen my faith. May seeking you and seeking the truth make your presence even more real in my life.

When doubts filled my mind, your comfort gave me renewed hope and cheer. . . . The LORD is my fortress; my God is the mighty rock where I hide. PSALM 94:19, 22

DAY 144

☼ A prayer about ENERGY
When I can't move forward

LORD,

My energy level is so low. I feel stuck, and I think I know why. Most of my energy is being wasted because I'm focused on things that have already happened. I'm dragging around baggage from my past, and it's a heavy load. It's draining me of energy I could be using for today's tasks and problems. But your Word tells me that I need to let go of the past. If there are sins I need to confess, reveal them to me so I may ask your forgiveness and move on. If I have hurt others, give me the courage to make it right. If I've made choices that I wish I could redo, help me to learn from my mistakes and let go of the regret. If others have hurt me, give me for the strength to forgive them and seek reconciliation. Teach me not to waste my time and energy on things I cannot change. Instead, show me how to move forward into the wonderful future you have for me.

I press on to possess that perfection for which Christ Jesus first possessed me. No, dear brothers and sisters, I have not achieved it, but I focus on this one thing: Forgetting the past and looking forward to what lies ahead, I press on to reach the end of the race and receive the heavenly prize for which God, through Christ Jesus, is calling us.
PHILIPPIANS 3:12-14

☼ A prayer about CHOICES
When I want to make the best decisions

LORD,

Each day I'm faced with many choices—how I should use my time, what goals I should pursue, what I should allow to influence me. I want to make good choices. Help me to remember that the best decisions I can make, no matter what the issue, are decisions that honor you and obey your Word. If I do that, I will be in the center of your will for my life. I know the way to make those best decisions is to read the Bible regularly, pray for guidance, and ask for help from godly friends and mentors. The better I know you, the easier it will be to honor you in what I do and say. Teach me, Lord, to put you before everything else in my life. It's a simple concept, but it's challenging to do. When I put you first, others second, and myself third, I know I'll find joy and satisfaction in following your ways. I know that each day I have a choice to serve you. May I always make the right choice.

Be very careful to obey all the commands and the instructions that Moses gave to you. Love the LORD your God, walk in all his ways, obey his commands, hold firmly to him, and serve him with all your heart and all your soul. JOSHUA 22:5

☼ A prayer about GOSSIP
When I am tempted to gossip

FATHER,

I have to admit that it's fun to gossip. I enjoy being in on the latest news. But too often when I'm sharing secrets with others, I know I'm not trying to build up the people I'm talking about. My intention may not be to damage their reputation, but if I'm honest I know that's what often happens. Forgive me, Lord. I want to honor you with my words. Guard my lips.

A troublemaker plants seeds of strife; gossip separates the best of friends. PROVERBS 16:28

DAY 147 *Prayerful Moment*

☼ A prayer about CHURCH
When I wonder how I can experience God at church

LORD,

I know your Holy Spirit lives in the heart of every believer. What a gift! Yet you also say that you live within the community of the church. When believers gather together, we meet you in a special way. Just as going to a live concert or sports event is much more exciting than watching it on TV, participating with other believers makes worshiping you much more meaningful. Help me to enter into corporate worship enthusiastically.

What joy for those who can live in your house, always singing your praises. PSALM 84:4

☀ A prayer about GOD'S PRESENCE
When I want to be more aware that God is with me

LORD,

I've staked my life on you—yet sometimes I go hours without even thinking about you. How can that be? I want to be more aware of your presence with me. I want my ears to be tuned to what you are saying to me. My will-power is weak, so I need help. Maybe I should put a note on my computer reminding me to pray every time I sit down to work. Or I could set a recurring alarm on my cell phone, and when it goes off, I could take time to review how you have been with me in the last hour and ask you to help me in the hour ahead. Whatever the method, please teach me to take time to listen to you. I don't want to be on autopilot, because that will never lead to growth. Help me to enter into conversation with you as I go about my daily activities. As I get to know you better and let you into more of my life, I know you will be working in my heart to transform me.

Come and listen to my counsel. I'll share my heart with you and make you wise. PROVERBS 1:23

☼ **A prayer about APATHY**
When I don't care about anything

GOD,

Apathy has settled in, and I'm just going through the motions. My passion and my sense of purpose are gone, and my motivation seems to be draining away. How can I stop it? I need to remember that one of Satan's lies is that following you and doing your work are nothing to be excited about. It's not true! I cling to the knowledge that only through following you will my life have meaning, energy, and purpose. Your Word tells me how I can combat apathy: through purposeful work, a thankful heart, and serving others. Help me, Lord, to use these tools to fight off feelings of apathy. Renew my focus on your purpose for my life, and fan the flames of anticipation in my heart so that I may be excited about the blessings you have in store for me.

Our great desire is that you will keep on loving others as long as life lasts, in order to make certain that what you hope for will come true. Then you will not become spiritually dull and indifferent. Instead, you will follow the example of those who are going to inherit God's promises because of their faith and endurance. HEBREWS 6:11-12

☼ A prayer about CHANGE
When I'm facing difficult changes

LORD OF ALL,

Sometimes I get excited about the changes ahead in my life. It's exciting to see different paths in front of me and wonder what great things could be in store. But sometimes change seems to be for the worse. Maybe I liked the way things were, but now everything is different, and it's disconcerting. Or maybe things have fallen apart completely and unexpectedly, and I'm at a loss to know where to go from here. Help me to remember that nothing takes you by surprise. You are Lord of the universe! Even something that feels unpredictable and traumatic to me doesn't trump your will. You can take the worst things in my life and use them for my good and your glory. I remember the story of Joseph, who was sold by his own brothers into slavery—a change that must have seemed unbearable to him. Yet through that terrible experience he became governor of Egypt, and you used him to save many people from starvation. Lord, I give you these difficult changes in my life. May you turn them into something wonderful in my life and the lives of those around me.

We know that God causes everything to work together for the good of those who love God and are called according to his purpose for them. ROMANS 8:28

☼ A prayer about CONTENTMENT
When I'm searching for satisfaction

LORD,

When I consider what would bring me contentment, I usually imagine either having every material thing I think I need to be happy or having all my life's plans unfold neatly, just the way I expect. But the reality of life is that neither of those things may ever come true. Teach me that true contentment has nothing to do with possessions or circumstances. After all, the apostle Paul was jailed, beaten, and shipwrecked—yet he said he could be content in all situations. Help me to understand that genuine contentment only comes from the love and peace you offer. It remains secure even when other things are taken away. I know that the more I meditate on your Word and remember the eternal blessings you provide, the more content I will be. Teach me to find my satisfaction in you. I've put my faith in Jesus, and that can never be taken away from me.

Not that I was ever in need, for I have learned how to be content with whatever I have. I know how to live on almost nothing or with everything. I have learned the secret of living in every situation, whether it is with a full stomach or empty, with plenty or little. For I can do everything through Christ, who gives me strength. PHILIPPIANS 4:11-13

DAY 152

☀ **A prayer about ETERNITY**
   When I need to cultivate an eternal perspective

LORD,

At times I wonder why I should bother living a godly life, when the results could be persecution and loss. It feels like I have to give up so many things that other people my age seem to enjoy. But I know that's the wrong perspective. Help me to remember, Lord, that as creator of the world, you alone know the best way to live. So when I try to obey you, I'm putting myself in a position to enjoy life the way it is meant to be enjoyed. My relationships will be more fulfilling because people will be able to trust me. My life will be happier because I'll avoid many of the consequences of sin. And I'll be more secure because I will know where I am going after I die. Thank you for these blessings. Keep this eternal perspective at the front of my mind so that it will shape my actions and attitudes to your glory.

What do you benefit if you gain the whole world but lose your own soul? Is anything worth more than your soul?
MARK 8:36-37

☼ A prayer about APOLOGY
When it's hard to apologize to others

MERCIFUL GOD,

It's so difficult for me to say "I'm sorry." I hate admitting my faults even to myself, much less humbling myself enough to confess them to someone else. Yet I know that a sincere apology is the first step in changing my behavior and committing to do the right thing from now on. Take away my pride, Lord, and change my heart so that I will be ready to apologize when I am wrong.

People who conceal their sins will not prosper, but if they confess and turn from them, they will receive mercy. PROVERBS 28:13

DAY 154 *Prayerful Moment*

☼ A prayer about COMPETITION
When I'm frustrated about losing

LORD GOD,

When I compete against someone else and lose, I get frustrated and upset—especially if I don't think I did my best. Help me to remember that while competitions may help me learn, the results don't last forever. Ultimately, the greatest victory I can achieve in life is gaining eternal life through faith in you. May I keep my eyes fixed on that goal. Then I will be able to handle other victories and defeats with more grace and humility.

Thank God! He gives us victory over sin and death through our Lord Jesus Christ. 1 CORINTHIANS 15:57

☼ A prayer about GOD'S HAND
When I wonder how God is working in my life

FATHER,

How do you work in my life? Throughout the Bible I read stories of you demonstrating your power through visible, miraculous signs. But in my heart, the evidence of your hand is much more subtle. I know that sometimes you work through events in my life to change my heart. Other times you speak to me through a still, quiet voice in my mind, or through a passage in your Word. Give me ears to hear your voice, Lord. I never want to miss communication from you. Help me to look for evidence of your hand in my life. Remind me that you are constantly molding me, shaping me in your image. You will never give up on me; you will keep working until the day Christ returns and my eternal life begins. You will faithfully make me the person you have created me to be!

I am certain that God, who began the good work within you, will continue his work until it is finally finished on the day when Christ Jesus returns. PHILIPPIANS 1:6

☼ A prayer about DESIRES
When I want to desire God above all else

LORD,

I know that I am motivated by the things I really want. Whether it be respect, a position of importance, or a new car, the things I desire show the priorities of my heart. The more I want something, the more likely I am to work hard to achieve that goal. But where do you fit into my desires? Your Word tells me that it's possible for humans to know and experience you, the God of the universe, in a personal way. What could be a more worthwhile goal than that? Oh Lord, I'm amazed that you desire a relationship with me. Teach me to desire you with all my heart. May knowing you be the surpassing goal of my life. May my desire for you shine through so clearly that others will be able to see it.

As the deer longs for streams of water, so I long for you, O God. I thirst for God, the living God. When can I go and stand before him? PSALM 42:1-2

☼ A prayer about GRIEF
When I wonder if I'll see my loved ones in heaven

LORD JESUS,

It's easy to go along in life without giving much thought to heaven—until you lose someone you love. I am grieving. Someone I love has died, and I feel sad and lost. I miss this person so much! I am clinging to your promises about heaven. You tell me in your Word that all who believe in you will live eternally. It gives me great hope to imagine seeing my loved one someday. How wonderful that will be! I'm so grateful that you are the resurrection and the life, Lord Jesus. You hold the final power over death. You will one day rule over a Kingdom with no sin, no sickness, no death. I can't wait for that day. Comfort me now with these promises. Teach me to cling to them in this time of grief, knowing that someday all my hopes will be fulfilled. I will see my loved one again, and I will see you face to face. That's what heaven is all about.

God's home is now among his people! He will live with them, and they will be his people. God himself will be with them. He will wipe every tear from their eyes, and there will be no more death or sorrow or crying or pain. All these things are gone forever. REVELATION 21:3-4

☼ A prayer about THE IMPOSSIBLE
When I wonder if God still acts in the world

LORD,

Sometimes I question if miracles really happen anymore. Do you work in our world the way you did in Bible times? Yet I know you are actively involved in my life. Give me eyes of faith, that I may appreciate all the amazing things you accomplish for me and around me each day: the gift of forgiveness, the change of seasons, the intricacies of the human body and its ability to heal, the exact conditions needed to support life on this earth, the birth of a baby. From a human perspective so many of these things are impossible, yet nothing is impossible for you, who spoke all creation into being. Oh Lord, as I look for the miracles around me, please strengthen my faith. I know that even when things look impossible to me, you can and will act for your glory and my good.

Now all glory to God, who is able, through his mighty power at work within us, to accomplish infinitely more than we might ask or think. Glory to him in the church and in Christ Jesus through all generations forever and ever! EPHESIANS 3:20-21

☼ **A prayer about ADVICE**
When I'm not sure I'm receiving wise advice

FATHER,

When I ask my friends for advice, often it seems like they tell me what I want to hear instead of telling me the truth. That's easy and comfortable, but it's not what's best for me. Please give me discernment, Lord. I know that sometimes I need to be convicted of my sin. I need others to tell me when they see me going down the wrong path. Thank you that your Word is always truthful. It can expose my thoughts, desires, and motives. Help me to seek out people who will share your Word with me when I need to hear it. When they give me godly advice that convicts me of sin, teach me to respond with repentance and a soft heart.

All Scripture is inspired by God and is useful to teach us what is true and to make us realize what is wrong in our lives. It corrects us when we are wrong and teaches us to do what is right. 2 TIMOTHY 3:16

☼ A prayer about DECISIONS
When I wonder if my decisions matter

FATHER GOD,

I make hundreds of decisions every day, and each one seems so trivial. Yet I know each decision puts me a little further down either the right or wrong path. I want to follow the road you have for me. When I'm making a wrong turn, please put barriers in my path. May I be sensitive to your leading so that I will recognize what I'm doing wrong, turn around, and go the right way. I want to follow you.

My steps have stayed on your path; I have not wavered from following you. PSALM 17:5

☼ A prayer about NEW BEGINNINGS
When I want a fresh start

LORD,

Yesterday was not a good day. I don't like the person I was—the words I said, the choices I made, the way I treated others. But I'm grateful that I can have a fresh start every day because your mercies are new every morning. Because of your forgiveness, I don't have to stay burdened by yesterday's failures or regrets. Thank you that I can experience your love anew each day.

Great is his faithfulness; his mercies begin afresh each morning. LAMENTATIONS 3:23

☼ A prayer about HUMILITY
When I need to be humble before God

LOVING GOD,

I think my concept of humility is wrong. I tend to think of a humble person as one who walks around with his head down and doesn't think he can do anything right. But that's not the way your Word talks about humility. Instead, humility seems to mean admitting that I need you, acknowledging my own sins, and seeking your forgiveness. When I'm struggling with pride, I'm unable to admit that I have flaws. I waste a lot of energy trying to prove to myself and others that I'm perfect. Please teach me that pursuing humility means being honest with myself and with you. It means giving you my whole heart without trying to hide or hold anything back. Show me that living with humility frees me from the exhausting task of keeping up appearances. As I live honestly and humbly before you, may I be open to being used by you.

As the Scriptures say, "God opposes the proud but favors the humble." So humble yourselves before God. Resist the devil, and he will flee from you. Come close to God, and God will come close to you. Wash your hands, you sinners; purify your hearts, for your loyalty is divided between God and the world. Let there be tears for what you have done. . . . Humble yourselves before the Lord, and he will lift you up in honor. JAMES 4:6-10

☼ A prayer about TALKING TO GOD
When I'm thankful for prayer

LORD,

I'm so grateful that you encourage me to pray. You invite me to come to you and praise you, make requests, confess sins, express my pain and frustration, ask for guidance, and simply share what is happening in my life. You welcome me into your presence. You tell me that you want to give me good gifts. What an incredible thing! May I never take this for granted. May I come to you in faith, with a soft heart, ready to speak and to listen.

Keep on asking, and you will receive what you ask for. Keep on seeking, and you will find. Keep on knocking, and the door will be opened to you. For everyone who asks, receives. Everyone who seeks, finds. And to everyone who knocks, the door will be opened. You parents—if your children ask for a loaf of bread, do you give them a stone instead? Or if they ask for a fish, do you give them a snake? Of course not! So if you sinful people know how to give good gifts to your children, how much more will your heavenly Father give good gifts to those who ask him. MATTHEW 7:7-11

⚙ A prayer about STATUS
When I am concerned about my position

LORD JESUS,

I waste a lot of energy thinking about status. How do I rank compared to other people? Do others look up to me? Am I smarter or more accomplished than my peers? Forgive me for making questions like these the focus of my attention. I need to learn that what the world says about status is not at all what you say. After all, you gave up everything to live on earth as a human, even your life—dying a criminal's death to pay for the sins of the world. Teach me that even if I am considered the most important, the smartest, the most attractive, or the most athletic, it's ultimately worth nothing unless I use that status for great purposes. May my aim be to build a good reputation that honors your name, to serve and bless other people, and to take opportunities to tell others about you. Help me to remember that it's when I use my status for your purposes rather than for my own goals that I will be truly blessed.

Many who are the greatest now will be least important then, and those who seem least important now will be the greatest then. MATTHEW 19:30

☼ A prayer about COMPROMISE
When I don't want to give in

HEAVENLY FATHER,

Sometimes I get stuck in a situation where I want my way, someone else wants hers, and neither one of us is going to give in. This can happen in my family, at work, at school, or with friends. I know that when I dig in my heels and refuse to budge, I'm really being selfish, and it just damages my relationships. In a situation where there's no right or moral answer, please help me have the humility to compromise. Teach me that one person doesn't have to win and the other person lose. If we each give a little, we'll both gain something and accomplish a greater good together. That's what compromise is really about. May I realize that compromise is a way I can show love, not selfishness, to those around me.

Make me truly happy by agreeing wholeheartedly with each other, loving one another, and working together with one mind and purpose. Don't be selfish; don't try to impress others. Be humble, thinking of others as better than yourselves. Don't look out only for your own interests, but take an interest in others, too. PHILIPPIANS 2:2-4

☼ **A prayer about MY HEART**
  When I want to pursue a pure heart

LORD,

Your Word tells me that I will harvest what I plant. Just as pumpkin seeds produce pumpkins and sunflower seeds produce sunflowers, so my heart will produce whatever I plant in it. I know that if I harbor negative thoughts or attitudes, they will come out in my actions and words. But that's not the kind of result I want! Instead, I want my life to produce good thoughts, motives, and actions. Purify my heart, Lord. I need your help to stay away from sinful thoughts. I want to honor you. I know that in this life I'll never be completely pure, but it's a goal I can pursue. May my desire for a clean heart and mind affect my relationships with you, with my family, and with my friends. And as I commit to pursuing a pure heart, may others see good fruit produced in my life.

Don't be misled—you cannot mock the justice of God. You will always harvest what you plant. Those who live only to satisfy their own sinful nature will harvest decay and death from that sinful nature. But those who live to please the Spirit will harvest everlasting life from the Spirit.
GALATIANS 6:7-8

☼ **A prayer about JOY**
When I hope for lasting joy

HEAVENLY FATHER,

I know you don't promise constant happiness. That's impossible in this mixed-up world. Yet you do promise lasting joy for all who follow you. I can experience joy despite my problems because I know that you will help me through them and that someday you will take them all away. Teach me to have an eternal perspective. Show me that even when I'm temporarily unhappy, I can still have lasting joy.

Always be full of joy in the Lord. I say it again—rejoice!
PHILIPPIANS 4:4

DAY 168 *Prayerful Moment*

☼ **A prayer about HOLINESS**
When I wonder what it means to be holy

HOLY GOD,

Your Word teaches that you have made all believers holy, set apart for a special purpose. I know this means being free from sin, which is only possible through your forgiveness. Yet it also means practicing righteousness, purity, and godliness. Help me to commit to this, Lord. Show me what it means to be set apart from the world. Please work in my life and make me holy.

Even before he made the world, God loved us and chose us in Christ to be holy and without fault in his eyes. EPHESIANS 1:4

☼ A prayer about ACCOMPLISHMENTS
When I want my efforts to be pleasing to God

HEAVENLY FATHER,

Too often I find myself thinking that if I do enough great things, other people will be impressed and will respect me. Then I even start thinking that I have to do great things to please you and to earn your love and forgiveness. Help me always to remember that I can't earn them—you have given them to me through your grace. You accepted me before I'd ever accomplished anything! You have called me and equipped me to serve you, but it's not about my own efforts. Teach me that my greatest accomplishment is allowing you to carry out your plans through me. May I let go of my need to be accepted because of my performance. Instead, may I be willing to let your power—not my gifts—show through what I do.

This Good News tells us how God makes us right in his sight. This is accomplished from start to finish by faith. As the Scriptures say, "It is through faith that a righteous person has life." ROMANS 1:17

☼ A prayer about COMMITMENT
When I need courage to keep my commitment to God

LORD,

Sometimes painful consequences come from obeying you. Other people might make fun of me, or I might lose out on an opportunity because I just don't fit in with everyone else. Someday I might even face stronger persecution. But if I'm committed to you, I need to be willing to accept those consequences. There will always be people who oppose you—and so they will oppose me when I stand up for your ways. Give me courage to stand firm. May I trust you to defend me instead of getting caught up in justifying myself. May I respond to others with grace and truth, even when they are angry or offensive. As I hold tightly to my commitment to you, may my words and actions reflect your character and so turn people to you. You are my Lord.

Trust in the LORD with all your heart; do not depend on your own understanding. Seek his will in all you do, and he will show you which path to take. PROVERBS 3:5-6

⚙ A prayer about PERFECTION
When perfectionism is holding me back

LORD,

Why do I feel that I have to do everything perfectly? Sometimes I do nothing because I'm afraid I will make a mistake. I don't take an opportunity because it might not be the perfect opportunity. I don't take a risk because I might fail. My perfectionism paralyzes me. I know that's not what you want for me. You don't want me to live in fear, and you don't expect me to do everything perfectly. Only you are perfect. Thank you that you work through imperfect people and circumstances. You can bring good from any situation—even my mistakes. Forgive me for being so caught up in myself and my performance that I stop trusting you and stop following you. Teach me, Lord, that I don't have to do things perfectly. All you ask is that I follow you in obedience. You will do the rest.

God has not given us a spirit of fear and timidity, but of power, love, and self-discipline. 2 TIMOTHY 1:7

☼ A prayer about CHARACTER
When I want to reflect God's character

LORD GOD,

You have called me to be one of your people—chosen by you, dedicated to you, and holy. As part of that calling, you ask me to model your character. You tell me that my character is a means of revealing yourself to the world. On my own, I fall so far short. But you don't ask me to do it on my own. In fact, you promise to work in my heart and transform me into your image. Thank you for always being with me. You give me the help I need to display characteristics like love, joy, peace, patience, kindness, goodness, faithfulness, gentleness, and self-control. Change me, Lord, so that others will see your character in me—and be drawn to you.

The Holy Spirit produces this kind of fruit in our lives: love, joy, peace, patience, kindness, goodness, faithfulness, gentleness, and self-control. There is no law against these things! . . . Since we are living by the Spirit, let us follow the Spirit's leading in every part of our lives. GALATIANS 5:22-23, 25

⚙ **A prayer about REST**
When I need rest

LORD,

When I am rushing around at every moment, trying to get through my to-do list, help me to remember that you want me to get rest. After all, you instituted a day of rest after Creation as an example for people to follow. Teach me to balance work and rest. Sometimes I have so much to do that I can't see the end of it, but working without a break only makes me more tired and anxious. Please give me the discipline to take the breaks I need to refresh my mind, my body, and my spirit. Show me that rest isn't just about stopping work and doing something mindless to pass the time. It means intentionally being still before you and letting you restore my joy and my perspective. May those moments with you refresh and inspire me, giving new energy and focus to my work.

The creation of the heavens and the earth and everything in them was completed. On the seventh day God had finished his work of creation, so he rested from all his work. And God blessed the seventh day and declared it holy, because it was the day when he rested from all his work of creation.

GENESIS 2:1-3

☼ A prayer about PANIC
When I need to find calm

LORD GOD,

Panic has overtaken me, and I feel physically and emotionally paralyzed. I'm overcome with worry and fear. This stress came so suddenly that I couldn't prepare for it, and I'm too frozen to know how to deal with it. Help me, Lord! I can't fix this on my own. I need you to rescue me. Grant me your peace that passes all understanding. Calm me and help me to know that you alone are in control.

Call on me when you are in trouble, and I will rescue you, and you will give me glory. PSALM 50:15

DAY 175 *Prayerful Moment*

☼ A prayer about CRITICISM
When I dislike receiving criticism

GOD,

I don't like receiving criticism, even constructive criticism. It hurts my pride to hear someone tell me what I did poorly and where I can do better. But I know that the only way to improve at something is to practice. And feedback from someone who's experienced, like a teacher, boss, or coach, will help me practice effectively. Teach me humility, Lord, that I may be able to learn from others. May my pride never get in the way of doing my best.

Listen to my instruction and be wise. Don't ignore it. PROVERBS 8:33

☼ A prayer about WEAKNESS
When I hope God can work through my weakness

LORD,

I feel weak and insignificant. All the challenges and demands I'm facing reveal the very weaknesses that I would like to hide. I try to appear strong, but I know my façade is developing cracks. I'm so flawed—yet you tell me you can demonstrate your power and wisdom even through my weaknesses. Teach me that true weakness is depending on my own strength, because it will never be sufficient. May I understand that genuine strength comes when I see my weaknesses as opportunities to allow your power to work through me.

[Paul said,] "I was given a thorn in my flesh. . . . Three different times I begged the Lord to take it away. Each time he said, 'My grace is all you need. My power works best in weakness.' So now I am glad to boast about my weaknesses, so that the power of Christ can work through me. That's why I take pleasure in my weaknesses, and in the insults, hardships, persecutions, and troubles that I suffer for Christ. For when I am weak, then I am strong."
2 CORINTHIANS 12:7-10

☼ A prayer about CRISIS
When I wonder if God is with me in times of crisis

FATHER,

In times of crisis, I sometimes catch myself praying that you would be with me. Yet when I think about it more clearly, I know you are already here. You have promised never to leave me or forsake me, and I'm so thankful for that reassurance. Help me instead to pray that I will recognize your presence and have the humility to accept your help. Your Word makes clear that you don't promise to prevent crisis in my life. This world is fallen, and terrible things sometimes happen. But you do promise to be with me and for me, helping me through any crisis I face. I cling to that promise, Lord. Please guide me toward peace and hope even in the midst of my struggles. And help me always to remember that your ultimate promise is to bring me to heaven, where all trouble and crisis will end forever.

God is our refuge and strength, always ready to help in times of trouble. So we will not fear when earthquakes come and the mountains crumble into the sea. Let the oceans roar and foam. Let the mountains tremble as the waters surge! PSALM 46:1-3

☀ **A prayer about NATURE**
 When I want to care for God's creation

CREATOR GOD,

You made this world, and you made it beautiful. I'm so glad you care not just about function but also about beauty. If you didn't, you wouldn't have created so many varieties of flowers, butterflies, and animals—not to mention mountains, rivers, oceans, and deserts. As I enjoy the beauty of your world, help me to care for it. Just as you asked Adam and Eve to care for the Garden of Eden, so you expect me to care for my little corner of the earth as well. May I be wise in the choices I make. Teach me to be a good steward of the environment because it is your creation and it proclaims your glory.

The heavens proclaim the glory of God. The skies display his craftsmanship. Day after day they continue to speak; night after night they make him known. They speak without a sound or word; their voice is never heard. Yet their message has gone throughout the earth, and their words to all the world. PSALM 19:1-4

☼ A prayer about GOALS
When I want to focus my attention on the right things

LORD,

The day can get away from me. I start out with good intentions and lofty goals, but by bedtime I've forgotten all of them and I'm just trying to get through the most urgent things on my to-do list. I need your help to focus each day on what's really important. Teach me to think about some key questions each morning: Will my plans today please you? How can I serve others today? Will what I'm doing today change me for better or for worse? I know that these questions will remind me to bring my focus back to you. Help me to keep you at the forefront of my mind as I make decisions each day about how to spend my time. At the end of the day, I want to know I have accomplished things that help others, glorify you, and strengthen my faith.

Do you have the gift of speaking? Then speak as though God himself were speaking through you. Do you have the gift of helping others? Do it with all the strength and energy that God supplies. Then everything you do will bring glory to God through Jesus Christ. All glory and power to him forever and ever! I PETER 4:11

☀ A prayer about WISDOM
When I want to become wise

GOD OF WISDOM,

I may pride myself on my intelligence and on the knowledge I've gained through school. Yet I know that intelligence and knowledge don't guarantee a balanced, productive, or fulfilling life. I need your wisdom to find success in relationships, to witness about my faith, to reach spiritual maturity, and to navigate the problems that will come my way. O Lord, please help me to recognize that I am ultimately accountable to you and fully dependent on you. That's the foundation of godly wisdom. As I grow in wisdom, I pray for a perspective that will penetrate the distorted messages of this world and show me the right way to go. Teach me to apply your truth and principles to my daily relationships and situations. May I depend on your wisdom to show me the difference between good and bad, right and wrong.

Fear of the LORD is the foundation of wisdom. Knowledge of the Holy One results in good judgment. Wisdom will multiply your days and add years to your life. If you become wise, you will be the one to benefit. If you scorn wisdom, you will be the one to suffer. PROVERBS 9:10-12

☼ A prayer about LOVING OTHERS
When I want to take action to love others

LORD GOD,

You have commanded me to love my neighbor. That can be inconvenient, but you don't let me off the hook just because it's hard. Your Word tells me to make the most of every opportunity to show your love to those who aren't believers. Please give me the courage to get involved in others' lives. May my loving actions give those around me a glimpse of you.

Live wisely among those who are not believers, and make the most of every opportunity. Let your conversation be gracious and attractive so that you will have the right response for everyone. COLOSSIANS 4:5-6

DAY 182 *Prayerful Moment*

☼ A prayer about DISCOURAGEMENT
When I am feeling down

LORD,

I am so discouraged. Nothing seems to be going my way. Sometimes it seems like everyone else has it together and I'm the only person who has troubles. Yet when I look past the surface, I know that's not true. Everyone has hurts and problems of some kind. Help me to remember that others are dealing with the same things I am. And what's more, you are with me through every moment. Thank you for that comfort.

The LORD is close to the brokenhearted; he rescues those whose spirits are crushed. PSALM 34:18

⚙ A prayer about BELONGING
When I wonder what it means to belong to God

HEAVENLY FATHER,

I am blessed to be part of your family. You have claimed
me, and I belong to you! Yet I'm not always sure what
this means for my life. When I look in your Word, I see
that part of belonging is obeying. Moses often reminded
the Israelites about the good things you had in store for
them if they were faithful in obeying you. When I follow your commands for life, I'm showing with my actions
how much I love you. Teach me that your commands are
given out of love, to protect me, guide me, and help me
experience life to the fullest. Thank you for welcoming me
into your family and showering me with blessings—such
as peace of mind, lasting joy, and the comfort of your presence. May I never forget how much love and satisfaction
come from belonging to you.

*If you obey the commands of the LORD your God and walk
in his ways, the LORD will establish you as his holy people as
he swore he would do. Then all the nations of the world will
see that you are a people claimed by the LORD, and they will
stand in awe of you.* DEUTERONOMY 28:9-10

☼ A prayer about PAIN
When I need relief from my hurts

LORD,

I'm dealing with a painful situation right now. Things aren't getting better, and I'm so discouraged. How can I begin to emerge from this dark place? I need your help. Please teach me that sometimes the answer comes in looking past myself. It's easy to be self-focused when I'm hurting so much, but help me to remember that other people may be hurting too. The opportunities you give me—to help someone in need, volunteer for a good cause, or write a note of encouragement to someone who is struggling even more than I am—may help me cope with my own sorrow. Show me how to look up from my own pain long enough to notice your comforting presence all around me. You promise me that sorrow won't get the last word. You will redeem my sorrow by fulfilling your promises of comfort and hope. Thank you, Lord.

Weeping may last through the night, but joy comes with the morning. . . . You have turned my mourning into joyful dancing. You have taken away my clothes of mourning and clothed me with joy, that I might sing praises to you and not be silent. O LORD my God, I will give you thanks forever! PSALM 30:5, 11-12

☀ A prayer about HYPOCRISY
When I want to do what I've promised

FATHER,

When I look at those around me who don't know you, I see that nothing turns them away from faith more than hypocrisy. Someone who pretends to be moral or kind but really is selfish or deceitful makes all believers look bad. Help me, Lord, always to be genuine. Keep me from pretending to be something I'm not just to get something I want. Teach me always to be sincere, honest, and humble, especially as I interact with unbelievers. Help me to examine myself and discover any areas where I am saying the right thing but not doing it. May I never lose others' trust because I've acted hypocritically.

Don't just listen to God's word. You must do what it says. Otherwise, you are only fooling yourselves. For if you listen to the word and don't obey, it is like glancing at your face in a mirror. You see yourself, walk away, and forget what you look like. But if you look carefully into the perfect law that sets you free, and if you do what it says and don't forget what you heard, then God will bless you for doing it.
JAMES 1:22-25

☼ A prayer about MOTIVES
When I wonder how much my motives matter

HEAVENLY FATHER,

It's tempting to think that only my outward actions matter. After all, if I do the right thing, what difference does it make if I'm doing it for the wrong reasons? But your Word tells me that's incorrect thinking. Teach me that my motives are as important as my actions, because selfish and sinful motives will eventually produce selfish and sinful actions. Others may look only at my behavior, but you look at my heart. I want to please you with my motives. Purify my heart so that I will not be motivated by selfish ambition or a desire to look good in front of others. May I do the right things for the right reasons—out of compassion for others, out of obedience, out of a desire to glorify you.

I know, my God, that you examine our hearts and rejoice when you find integrity there. You know I have done all this with good motives. I CHRONICLES 29:17

☼ **A prayer about APOLOGY**
 When I need to apologize

FATHER,

Sometimes I know I've hurt someone else—a friend, a class-mate, a parent, or even you—but I just can't make myself apologize. I want to look good in front of others, and I feel too proud to admit that I did something wrong. But I'm starting to realize that pride can have terrible effects on my relationships. Humble me, Lord. Soften my heart so I will be willing to apologize. I know that confession and repentance can open the door to healing and blessing. Teach me to acknowledge my faults, ask for forgiveness, and do whatever I can to make things right. I know you are willing to wipe the slate clean and forgive me.

The high and lofty one who lives in eternity, the Holy One, says this: "I live in the high and holy place with those whose spirits are contrite and humble. I restore the crushed spirit of the humble and revive the courage of those with repentant hearts." ISAIAH 57:15

⚙ **A prayer about EMPATHY**
When I want to be a better friend

LOVING GOD,
Teach me to respond with empathy to those around me. When my friends are joyful, let me rejoice with them, celebrating their successes without jealousy. When my friends are grieving, let me grieve with them, sharing their sorrows and comforting them as best I can. Help me to put my own feelings aside in those moments to put myself in the shoes of my friends. May they see your love in me.

Be happy with those who are happy, and weep with those who weep. Live in harmony with each other. ROMANS 12:15-16

DAY 189 *Prayerful Moment*

⚙ **A prayer about WORRY**
When I need to turn my anxieties over to God

LORD JESUS,
I know I can trust you to take care of me, yet you never promised that my life would be problem-free. Teach me not to be surprised or frightened by hard times. Keep me from borrowing trouble by worrying about things that may never happen. Instead, let me turn my worries to you and receive your peace in return. You are with me, and you are faithful.

The LORD keeps watch over you as you come and go, both now and forever. PSALM 121:8

☼ A prayer about GOD'S POWER
When I need God's strength

MIGHTY GOD,

When I am weak, I am thankful that you don't just tell me to imitate your strength. Trying my best wouldn't get me very far. Instead, you have given me your Holy Spirit! You are working through me and helping me to grow strong. Thank you for providing me with your armor, which protects me and gives me the power I need to stand against the schemes of the devil. Help me always to remember that you have equipped me to do your work. When a problem comes up, teach me to look not at the size of the problem but at your strength. With your help I can do mighty things.

A final word: Be strong in the Lord and in his mighty power. Put on all of God's armor so that you will be able to stand firm against all strategies of the devil. For we are not fighting against flesh-and-blood enemies, but against evil rulers and authorities of the unseen world, against mighty powers in this dark world, and against evil spirits in the heavenly places. EPHESIANS 6:10-12

☼ A prayer about GENEROSITY
When I want to give to God

LORD,

You have given me so much. I may not be as wealthy as the richest in this country, but compared to many around the world, I have everything I need. I pray for a generous heart, that I will learn to love giving to others. When I give, teach me to focus not on what I'm giving up but on what others will gain. Give me eyes to see places where I can make a difference. Maybe the money I give can provide books for someone trying to go to school or can help to pay even a little of a pastor's salary. Maybe I can donate clothes to someone who can use them, or perhaps I can give of my time to tutor a struggling student. Thank you that there are so many ways to give, even if I don't have a lot of money right now. Keep me from using that as an excuse. Impress on my heart that it is more blessed to give than to receive.

While Jesus was in the Temple, he watched the rich people dropping their gifts in the collection box. Then a poor widow came by and dropped in two small coins. "I tell you the truth," Jesus said, "this poor widow has given more than all the rest of them. For they have given a tiny part of their surplus, but she, poor as she is, has given everything she has."
LUKE 21:1-4

☼ A prayer about TEAMWORK
When it's difficult to be part of a team

GOD,
Sometimes I really don't like being part of a team. It feels easier to do things by myself than to negotiate with other people or have to solve conflicts. But I know that's the wrong attitude when it comes to work for your Kingdom. The job is much too big for one person! You have given all believers the mission of making disciples of all nations, and that's a huge task. Please help me to welcome other people who want to work with me. Teach me to be open to their ideas and supportive of their efforts. Remind me that teamwork is most effective with others who share my goals and values—so working with other believers to share the gospel or serve people in your name is the best kind of teamwork of all.

Two people are better off than one, for they can help each other succeed. If one person falls, the other can reach out and help. But someone who falls alone is in real trouble. . . . A person standing alone can be attacked and defeated, but two can stand back-to-back and conquer. Three are even better, for a triple-braided cord is not easily broken.
ECCLESIASTES 4:9-10, 12

☼ A prayer about SPIRITUAL DRYNESS
When I feel dry and empty

O LORD,

My soul is so dry, and I'm thirsting for something that will be truly fulfilling. I know I'm in this season of drought because I'm feeling pressured and am undergoing temptation. My desire to know you and serve you seems to have dried up completely. How do I revive it? Teach me to take extra care of my soul during this time. May I keep watering it with your Word. Please revive me with a sense of renewed purpose and passion. Refresh me, Lord. Help me to keep my focus not on my sense of emptiness but on you. When I remember your character—your love, your patience, your holiness, your wisdom—I know my sense of excitement will return. Help me to persevere, knowing that you can and will restore my joy.

The LORD will guide you continually, giving you water when you are dry and restoring your strength. You will be like a well-watered garden, like an ever-flowing spring. ISAIAH 58:11

⚙ A prayer about DISAGREEMENT
When others disagree with me

LORD,

I know it's impossible for people to agree all the time. Why would we even want that? It would be boring if everyone thought the same way. Yet sometimes I feel uncomfortable when I disagree with those around me, because it's easy for me to become angry or defensive. I need your help to handle those disagreements in a godly way. Teach me first to try to understand how others arrived at their position. Keep me from belittling them or making fun of their ideas. Instead, help me to treat them respectfully and try to find common ground. Give me creativity to find solutions that will work. Even if we can't agree, keep me from pointless arguing. May I always respond with respect and kindness so that relationships can remain intact.

Pursue righteous living, faithfulness, love, and peace. Enjoy the companionship of those who call on the Lord with pure hearts. Again I say, don't get involved in foolish, ignorant arguments that only start fights. A servant of the Lord must not quarrel but must be kind to everyone . . . and be patient with difficult people. 2 TIMOTHY 2:22-24

☼ A prayer about COURAGE
When I need to move ahead in spite of fear

FATHER,

I need courage to face some of the things in front of me today. Help me to remember that having courage doesn't mean that I'm not afraid. Instead, it means that fear will not paralyze me. Please give me the confident assurance that I can succeed at the tasks ahead. Give me the courage to stand firm against evil, remain strong in the faith, resist temptation, and do the right thing.

Jesus spoke to them at once. "Don't be afraid," he said. "Take courage! I am here!" MARK 6:50

DAY 196 *Prayerful Moment*

☼ A prayer about WORDS
When I need to be careful about what I say

LOVING GOD,

I know that my words have consequences. Teach me that angry or impatient words may inflict wounds on someone else, while helpful words may encourage others or even move someone a step closer to you. Before I speak, remind me to stop and think about what the consequences of my words might be. May I speak in a way that reflects your character.

You must all be quick to listen, slow to speak, and slow to get angry. JAMES 1:19

☀ **A prayer about DISCONTENTMENT**
When I am caught up in what I want

LORD,

The more time I spend trying to attain more things, the more discontented I feel. How can that be? I think it's because when my focus is on getting more, I get caught up in jealousy and comparing what I have to what others have. Help me to understand the difference between needs and wants. Teach me that when I have all that I really need—food, water, shelter, and love—I can be content. Help me to recognize that it's through your provision that my needs are met. You always know exactly what I need. Since you are generous to me, I don't have to grab tightly to what I have. Teach me to have a loose grasp on my possessions and to share generously with others as well.

At the moment I have all I need—and more! . . . And this same God who takes care of me will supply all your needs from his glorious riches, which have been given to us in Christ Jesus. PHILIPPIANS 4:18-19

☼ **A prayer about LEARNING**
When I need a reminder that learning is worthwhile

LORD GOD,

It's been easy to take school for granted or even think of it as boring drudgery. But I'm thankful for the opportunity I've had to get an education. The things I've learned can give me greater insight into how your world works, and I know you will use the knowledge I've gained for your purposes. Maybe you're preparing me for something in my future that I can't even see yet! Help me to take advantage of the opportunities I have and continue to learn as much as I can. May I make the most of where I am right now so that I can make the most of wherever you place me in the future.

*Tune your ears to wisdom, and concentrate on under-
standing. Cry out for insight, and ask for understanding.
Search for them as you would for silver; seek them like
hidden treasures. Then you will understand what it
means to fear the LORD, and you will gain knowledge
of God.* PROVERBS 2:2-5

☼ A prayer about DEPRESSION
When I am struggling

LORD,

I can feel myself sinking into discouragement. It's like I have tunnel vision. All I can see are my own problems, pain, and despair. I'm withdrawing into myself, and I know I'm losing perspective. Help me, Lord! Free me from this self-obsession and turn my focus outward again. Teach me that one way I can stop this downward spiral is to make an effort to praise you for everything I can think of: your greatness, your love, your holiness, your faithfulness, all you have done for me, how valuable I am to you. May remembering these things renew my mind and help me appreciate all the wonderful things about my life. Show me also that reaching out to others and offering help and comfort may draw my focus away from myself and help me gain a more accurate perspective on life. I'm so grateful that you care for me even in these times of depression and discouragement.

All praise to God, the Father of our Lord Jesus Christ. God is our merciful Father and the source of all comfort. He comforts us in all our troubles so that we can comfort others. When they are troubled, we will be able to give them the same comfort God has given us. 2 CORINTHIANS 1:3-4

☼ **A prayer about PURPOSE**
When I wonder why I'm here

ALL-KNOWING GOD,

I feel dissatisfied. I'm longing for something, and I'm not entirely sure what it is. I want to find significance. I want to fill a spot that is uniquely suited to me, to meet a need that no one else can meet. I want to find my purpose for life! But when I wonder how I will ever do this, I remember that you are the one who knows me better than I know myself. You know what will fulfill me. You know exactly what will satisfy the longings of my heart. Teach me to seek your guidance for my life. Lord, lead me to the place where my longings and abilities meet in a way that advances your Kingdom and serves others. When I trust that you know me and that you are in control, my anxiety goes away. I know you want the best for me and that you will direct me.

You made all the delicate, inner parts of my body and knit me together in my mother's womb. Thank you for making me so wonderfully complex! . . . You saw me before I was born. Every day of my life was recorded in your book. Every moment was laid out before a single day had passed. How precious are your thoughts about me, O God. They cannot be numbered! PSALM 139:13-14, 16-17

☼ **A prayer about LONELINESS**
  When my friendships have failed

HEAVENLY FATHER,

I am hurt because some of my relationships have failed. I thought these people were my loyal friends, but then things fell apart and I have been left alone. I'm feeling sorry for myself right now, but I don't want to become bitter. Help me to turn to you, Lord. I know that you are the best friend of all because you are always loyal, always truthful, always loving. Let me experience your faithfulness now in this time of loneliness. As I do, teach me to be faithful to others, even when they abandon me. Give me courage to get involved with other people again. I know that will take the focus off my lonely feelings and direct it toward someone else's well-being. Guide me to places where I can get to know other people. Please bless me with good friends who will stay by me, encourage me, and draw me closer to you. May I be that kind of friend to them as well.

A real friend sticks closer than a brother. PROVERBS 18:24

☼ A prayer about WORSHIP
When I want to worship God better

LORD,

You created humans to worship you—to acknowledge that you are above everything else in the universe. You alone are worthy of worship, because you are almighty God! Teach me to worship by recognizing who you are and who I am in relation to you. Direct my priorities. You are my only source of lasting hope and joy, and I want to honor you with my life.

Everything comes from him and exists by his power and is intended for his glory. All glory to him forever!
ROMANS 11:36

DAY 203 *Prayerful Moment*

☼ A prayer about GOD'S CALL
When I wonder what God is calling me to do

LORD,

I long to be part of something big—bigger than just my own desires. I want to do something significant with my life. I believe you are calling me, Lord, to discover how I can serve you. Where is my unique place? Give me ears to listen to your call, whether it comes through your Word, through the advice of other believers, or simply through a task I find in front of me. Teach me to use my life meaningfully.

God's gifts and his call can never be withdrawn.
ROMANS 11:29

☀ **A prayer about SUFFERING**
When I wonder if anything good can come from suffering

LORD GOD,

I try to avoid suffering as much as possible, and I don't think I'm alone. Adversity challenges me physically, mentally, emotionally, and spiritually—I find it unpleasant and exhausting. Yet the truth is, it's through suffering that I grow. Teach me that the trials I face can make me stronger and wiser. The painful and difficult times in my life can strengthen my character and my faith. Don't let this pain be wasted, Lord. Please use it to change my perspective and turn my thoughts toward heaven. Strengthen my faith as I wait expectantly for your promises to be fulfilled. Help me trust that someday I will be able to look back and appreciate the ways I was refined by suffering.

We can rejoice, too, when we run into problems and trials, for we know that they help us develop endurance. And endurance develops strength of character, and character strengthens our confident hope of salvation. And this hope will not lead to disappointment. For we know how dearly God loves us, because he has given us the Holy Spirit to fill our hearts with his love. ROMANS 5:3-5

A prayer about STRESS
When I need help to cope with my stress

HEAVENLY FATHER,

I'm trying to do so much, but stuff is starting to fall through the cracks. Between work, friends, family, and activities at church, I just can't keep up. I'm constantly worried about letting someone down, forgetting something, or failing at one of my tasks. I need your help, Lord. How can I cope with this stress? Teach me that only you can give me genuine rest from all my stress and worries. Help me to come to you and lay my burdens at your feet. Show me that my identity is secure in you, that you love me no matter what. It's great to accomplish fantastic things or be known as the church's number one volunteer, but I realize that doing these things won't win favor with you or make you love me more than you already do. Please give me the right perspective on everything I'm trying to accomplish. Help me approach my busyness from a place of peace and security in your love, rather than constantly trying to prove myself. Then I'll know better which things I really need to focus on, and I'll be better able to handle them. I'm so grateful for your constant love!

[Jesus said,] "Come to me, all of you who are weary and carry heavy burdens, and I will give you rest."
MATTHEW 11:28

☼ A prayer about RESPONSIBILITY
When I feel stuck in my bad habits

LORD,

If I listen to the voices around me in this world, I start to think that I am a victim who has no power to resist temptation. My culture encourages me to think that my genes, environment, or circumstances excuse me from responsibility. It's tempting to think this way, because then when I mess up, I can shrug and say it wasn't really my fault. But that isn't what I want. If I'm a victim, I may not have to face responsibility, but I'll also be stuck in my bad habits and sins. Lord, I know that you have not created me to be a victim! I am not a slave to my sinful desires because you have freed me. You have taken control of my life, and you are more powerful than anything or anyone else. Teach me to take responsibility for the things I do. Help me to learn from my mistakes, turn away from my sins, and choose to follow you.

Do not let sin control the way you live; do not give in to sinful desires. Do not let any part of your body become an instrument of evil to serve sin. Instead, give yourselves completely to God, for you were dead, but now you have new life. So use your whole body as an instrument to do what is right for the glory of God. Sin is no longer your master, for you no longer live under the requirements of the law. Instead, you live under the freedom of God's grace.
ROMANS 6:12-14

☼ A prayer about THE IMPOSSIBLE
When I wonder how powerful God really is

LORD,

When I doubt your power, remind me that your Word is filled with stories of you doing the impossible. A sea is parted so your people can walk through safely, the sun keeps shining until a battle is won, a man survives three days in the belly of a fish, and a virgin gives birth to a baby boy. These stories defy logic! Yet because I trust your Word, I believe they are true. Help me to remember that you, the Creator of all things, can alter what you have created. You can break natural law and cause something supernatural to happen. I pray for more faith so I can understand that what I see with my eyes is not all there is. Nothing is impossible for you.

This is what the LORD of Heaven's Armies says: All this may seem impossible to you now, a small remnant of God's people. But is it impossible for me? says the LORD of Heaven's Armies. ZECHARIAH 8:6

☀ A prayer about PANIC
When I am experiencing anxiety

GOD OF PEACE,

Once in a while I have a moment of absolute panic. It can come when my circumstances are stressful, and it overwhelms me. It's a terrible feeling of paralyzing fear. In those moments, please help me to remember that you, the God of peace, are with me. Teach me to let go of what I cannot control, knowing that you are in control. Teach me to stop trying to rescue myself, knowing that you are here to rescue me. Remind me that my troubles are opportunities to turn to you and experience your peace, which is beyond all understanding. O God, may my security always be anchored in the knowledge that you are in control of my soul and my circumstances. May that knowledge dissolve the panic and bring me the peace that only you can provide.

Don't worry about anything; instead, pray about everything. Tell God what you need, and thank him for all he has done. Then you will experience God's peace, which exceeds anything we can understand. His peace will guard your hearts and minds as you live in Christ Jesus.
PHILIPPIANS 4:6-7

☀ A prayer about VULNERABILITY
When I am afraid to open up to others

LORD,

What would happen if other people knew who I really am, deep down inside? That thought scares me. I'm afraid of rejection, so I tend to keep my heart from others. That protects me, but it also isolates me because I can never let down my guard completely. Please give me the courage to be vulnerable and the wisdom to choose carefully those to whom I will reveal my heart.

Confess your sins to each other and pray for each other.
JAMES 5:16

DAY 210 *Prayerful Moment*

☀ A prayer about AGGRAVATION
When I wonder how to respond to aggravation

FATHER,

When I'm frustrated with another person, teach me to step back before I respond. Help me to take a minute to relax, figure out what is causing my strong reaction, and ask myself if it's really worth this much turmoil. I need your help to watch my words and curtail my anger. Keep me from starting an ugly cycle of hurt with someone else. I want to choose to do the right thing and respond in love.

"Don't sin by letting anger control you." Don't let the sun go down while you are still angry, for anger gives a foothold to the devil. EPHESIANS 4:26-27

☼ A prayer about FEELINGS
When I need help responding to my strong feelings

LORD GOD,

I'm tired of being ruled by my feelings. One minute I'm up and the next minute I'm down. I get tied up in knots about things that really shouldn't matter, and I lash out in anger when I'm feeling defensive. I need to be reminded that my feelings aren't a reliable guide to the truth. They're so easily influenced by the highs and lows of daily life, plus my own sinful nature, that they change all the time. It's not wrong to have strong emotions, but when I let them affect my words and actions, they sometimes get out of control. I need your Holy Spirit to take charge of my emotions, Lord. Help me to give the control over to you. As I do that and check my reactions against your Word, I know I'll have greater confidence to deal with whatever comes my way.

Let the Holy Spirit guide your lives. Then you won't be doing what your sinful nature craves. The sinful nature wants to do evil, which is just the opposite of what the Spirit wants. And the Spirit gives us desires that are the opposite of what the sinful nature desires. These two forces are constantly fighting each other, so you are not free to carry out your good intentions. But when you are directed by the Spirit, you are not under obligation to the law of Moses. GALATIANS 5:16-18

DAY 212

☼ A prayer about MY BEST
When I wonder why I should give my best to God

LORD,

I say you are first in my life, but too often my actions and my schedule don't reflect that. Giving you the leftovers of my money shows that I value money more than you. Spending time with you only when it's convenient shows that I value my own schedule more than time with you. O God, you have given me so much—most importantly salvation and eternal life through the death and resurrection of your Son! I never want to take those gifts for granted, yet I do almost every day by the way I choose to use my time and money. Forgive me, Lord, and change my heart. Help me to realize that giving my best to you will energize me and draw me closer to you. When I give to you first from my income, I'll be blessed with excitement as I see how you provide for me and how my money helps others. When I give you my time to serve others, I'll be blessed with peace in my relationships. May I always give my best to you.

"Bring all the tithes into the storehouse so there will be enough food in my Temple. If you do," says the LORD of Heaven's Armies, "I will open the windows of heaven for you. I will pour out a blessing so great you won't have enough room to take it in! Try it! Put me to the test!" MALACHI 3:10

☼ A prayer about ENCOURAGEMENT
When I am facing a daunting task

HEAVENLY FATHER,

I'm facing a difficult task, and I'm not sure I'm up for the challenge. Doubts are creeping in. Can I really accomplish something meaningful? How I need encouragement! Thank you, God, that you can strengthen me. You give me the courage to go on, and you renew my commitment and resolve. You give me hope that my task is not in vain, that I can make a difference. As I read your Word, I'm amazed by your strong words of comfort and encouragement to Joshua, a man who was about to take over from Moses, the most revered leader the Israelites ever had. That couldn't have been easy, but you told him you would always be with him, actively helping him. I know that's true for me, too. Teach me that I won't find encouragement by looking to myself or my circumstances. I will find it only by looking to you, my Sovereign God.

[The Lord] said, "Moses my servant is dead. Therefore, the time has come for you to lead these people, the Israelites, across the Jordan River into the land I am giving them. I promise you what I promised Moses: 'Wherever you set foot, you will be on land I have given you.' . . . No one will be able to stand against you as long as you live. For I will be with you as I was with Moses. I will not fail you or abandon you." JOSHUA 1:1-3, 5

☼ A prayer about HELP
When I wonder how God can help me

LORD,

When things are going badly, I sometimes wonder where you are. Are you really with me when I need you most? I know the answer is yes. You don't promise to save me from trouble—in fact, you tell me that I will have trouble in this life because this world is fallen and sinful. But your Word makes clear that you will never leave me, no matter what. Help me never to treat you like a genie in a bottle. You're not here to grant my wishes and do things the way I want. If you were, my faith would never grow. Instead of preventing the hard times, you help me through them. As I go through this tough time, please give me wisdom to cope, strength to endure, and discernment to overcome adversity. Teach me to rely on you. May my first reaction in trouble be to turn to you, trusting that you will be near to help me.

When you go through deep waters, I will be with you. When you go through rivers of difficulty, you will not drown. When you walk through the fire of oppression, you will not be burned up; the flames will not consume you. ISAIAH 43:2

☀ **A prayer about APPEARANCE**
   When I want to see beyond appearance

FATHER,

It's so easy to get caught up in the way I look. So many voices around me tell me that being attractive is the most important thing in life and that I should devote my time and energy to improving my appearance. I'm encouraged to evaluate others and choose my friends based on how they look. Yet I know that my body, face, and clothes only reflect my outward shell. My soul and character are what reflect my inner being, which will never age or die. Help me to remember that what I really am is inside, not outside. Teach me that walking with you will help me to reflect your beauty—your perfect character. That's what I want others to see when they look at me. Keep me, too, from judging others based only on the external. May I have eyes to see the real person within.

The LORD doesn't see things the way you see them. People judge by outward appearance, but the LORD looks at the heart. 1 SAMUEL 16:7

☼ A prayer about MOTIVATION
When I want to reclaim my enthusiasm for God's work

LORD,

Through your power at work within me, you give me opportunities to make an impact for eternity. You have a purpose for my life. You call me to work alongside you to advance your Kingdom, which encompasses everything good and right. What a privilege! May this wonderful truth stay fresh in my heart and motivate me every day.

[God] has invited you into partnership with his Son, Jesus Christ our Lord. 1 CORINTHIANS 1:9

DAY 217 *Prayerful Moment*

☼ A prayer about PLANS
When I want to make plans that are in line with God's will

LORD GOD,

I have lots of dreams for my life, but I want to make sure that they fit with your plans for me. Teach me to search your Word for the guidance you have revealed there. I know that anything that contradicts the Bible isn't in your will for me. Help me to walk step-by-step with you in faith, trusting you to show me the next step. May I always be aware of how much I need your leading.

You can make many plans, but the LORD's purpose will prevail. PROVERBS 19:21

⚙ **A prayer about CULTURE**
When I wonder how my culture affects me

HEAVENLY FATHER,

I'm so used to my culture that I don't always think about the impact it has on me. But just as the weather affects the clothes I wear, the activities I choose to do, and even my mood, so my culture affects me more than I realize. Help me to be aware of the ways it can influence my values, beliefs, and actions. I know that sometimes it takes on a life of its own, pressuring me to conform, challenging what I believe, and even making me feel embarrassed about the ways I don't fit in. I need your discernment so I can tell if I am making choices that are disappointing to you. I don't want to be indistinguishable from the surrounding culture, Lord. I want to be set apart for you. I know you can challenge my worldview and change the way I respond to my culture. May I be open to your transforming work in my heart.

Don't copy the behavior and customs of this world, but let God transform you into a new person by changing the way you think. Then you will learn to know God's will for you, which is good and pleasing and perfect. ROMANS 12:2

☼ **A prayer about ENEMIES**
When I wonder how I can love my enemies

LOVING GOD,

Showing love to my enemies seems completely unreasonable. If they don't like me and they aren't kind to me, why should I love them? But I'm reminded that I was once your enemy. I was caught in sin and acting in opposition to you—but then I found your grace and you forgave me. Help me, Lord, to see my enemies as you see them: as people in need of grace and forgiveness. I can't get to that point on my own. Left to myself, I often keep replaying their unkind words and actions in my mind, making myself more and more angry. I need you to work in my heart. Teach me to pray for those who are unkind to me, because I know that praying for them will cause me to feel compassion. Eventually I will care enough to want the best for them. With your grace, God, one of these enemies might become my friend.

All of you should be of one mind. Sympathize with each other. Love each other as brothers and sisters. Be tender-hearted, and keep a humble attitude. Don't repay evil for evil. Don't retaliate with insults when people insult you. Instead, pay them back with a blessing. That is what God has called you to do, and he will bless you for it.
1 PETER 3:8-9

☼ A prayer about PATIENCE
When it's hard to be patient with those around me

HEAVENLY FATHER,

Sometimes I get so impatient with the people around me! It seems that when I'm ready to move quickly, they drag their feet. When I need quiet, they want to talk. When I am busy, they need something from me. But when I start thinking like this, I know it's because I'm looking at life in a very self-centered way. Forgive me for thinking that everyone else's lives should revolve around mine. Give me humility, Lord. Teach me to consider others' needs as well as or even above my own. Increase my patience, compassion, and understanding for those I come into contact with each day. When I find myself getting impatient, remind me to consider the situation from the other person's perspective and respond in love.

Always be humble and gentle. Be patient with each other, making allowance for each other's faults because of your love.
EPHESIANS 4:2

☼ A prayer about LIMITATIONS
When I am aware of my faults

HEAVENLY FATHER,

Right now I'm so aware of my limitations—of all the things I can't do. I'm not the smartest or the fastest or the most attractive. So where do I fit in? Why would you use me? When I'm feeling discouraged, turn me toward your Word. Help me to remember the story of Gideon, who saw himself as weak, afraid, and the least of the least. Yet your angel greeted him as a "mighty hero"! He was more than he appeared to be, because you were ready to call out the best in him. You will call out the best in me, too. Thank you for seeing more in me than I see in myself. I see my limitations, but you see my potential—the person you created me to be. Teach me to see from your perspective, Lord. May I never hide because of my limitations. Rather, let me come before you as I am and let you mold me and use me for your glory.

Gideon son of Joash was threshing wheat at the bottom of a winepress to hide the grain from the Midianites. The angel of the LORD appeared to him and said, "Mighty hero, the LORD is with you!" . . . "But Lord," Gideon replied, "how can I rescue Israel? My clan is the weakest in the whole tribe of Manasseh, and I am the least in my entire family!" JUDGES 6:11-12, 15

☼ A prayer about PASSION
When I have lost my excitement for following God

LORD GOD,

I feel as if I'm drifting away from you. I'm tired, and I know I haven't been putting much effort into my relationship with you. Thank you that you never drift away from me. You are always fully committed to me. May I have that same commitment to you. I want to be excited again about the blessings you have given me and the ones you have promised for the future. Help me to be diligent as I try to know you better through studying your Word and talking to you in prayer. Teach me also to cultivate a thankful heart, since looking for opportunities to be thankful will change my attitude and help me realize how many wonderful things you do in my life. May I also serve others to the best of my ability, because that will remind me that I have a purpose and can do something good in this world. As I do all of these things, please make my apathy disappear. Then I'll have renewed passion for the purpose you have for my life.

Put on your new nature, and be renewed as you learn to know your Creator and become like him. COLOSSIANS 3:10

☼ A prayer about RESPONSIBILITY
When I want to show responsibility

LORD GOD,

I want to be known as a dependable person—someone others can count on to do what I say I will. Teach me to discern what needs to be done and then to follow through and see that it happens. Help me to be consistent in what I say and do. I know that when I handle small responsibilities, I'm more likely to be trusted with more. Please stretch me as I strive to become more reliable.

To those who use well what they are given, even more will be given, and they will have an abundance. MATTHEW 25:29

☼ A prayer about COMMANDMENTS
When I feel hemmed in by your commands

GOD,

When I drive on a curvy mountain road, I'm grateful for the guardrail next to me. It's not there to inhibit my freedom but to save my life. Help me to view your commandments the same way, Lord. They are intended not to limit me but to help me avoid danger. If I follow them, I will stay secure on the right path; my life won't go out of control.

The commandments of the LORD are right, bringing joy to the heart. The commands of the LORD are clear, giving insight for living. PSALM 19:8

⚙ **A prayer about REWARDS**
   When I wonder if God really will reward me for
   following him

LORD,

Thank you for blessing me with earthly and heavenly rewards. I know this kind of blessing doesn't mean that my life on earth will be smooth or that I'll be wealthy, but it does mean that I will benefit from following you. Teach me that when I obey you, I'm often protected from the evil I could get entangled in. When I do what you ask, you lead me on the right path to find more of your blessings, and you direct me into service that will please you and others. Thank you for the spiritual rewards you give as well—the amazing gift of salvation and eternal life; the blessing of a relationship with you, my Creator; the treasure of your Word; and the wonderful character traits of godliness, truth, wisdom, and a good reputation. May I always remember that these are the best rewards anyone could ask for, because they are lasting and priceless.

There truly is a reward for those who live for God; surely
there is a God who judges justly here on earth. PSALM 58:11

☼ A prayer about WORDS
When I wonder what impact my words have on others

GOD,

I know I take my words too lightly sometimes. I say whatever comes to mind without always being careful that it's true, kind, or necessary. But when I remember the impact others' language has had on me, both positive and negative, I realize how important it is to choose my words carefully. My tongue is a powerful tool, and I don't want to use it to hurt others. Teach me to use my words to encourage, inspire, comfort, and challenge others. May I stop myself from uttering words that are demeaning, insulting, annoying, or simply useless. I know the words I use reflect what is in my heart, so please continue to work in my life to make me more like you. I want my language to express love and grace to others.

Don't use foul or abusive language. Let everything you say be good and helpful, so that your words will be an encouragement to those who hear them. EPHESIANS 4:29

☀ **A prayer about COMPASSION**
When I need God to touch my heart

LORD JESUS,

Today my heart is hard. I see the needs around me, but I'm not responding in kindness. I find myself walking by hurting people, unable or unwilling to enter into their struggles. What is wrong? I know I'm too focused on myself—so much that I can't see beyond my problems to others' pain. I keep myself at a distance from anyone who might disturb my status quo. Yet I'm afraid that if I keep going this way, I'll be in danger of developing a heart of stone that's unresponsive either to you or to others. I don't want that, Lord. I want to love others as you love me. Please work in me and transform me. Stir up compassion for others that will melt my hard heart and compel me to action. I want to be your hands and feet in the world, sharing your love with those around me.

[Jesus said,] "Now I am giving you a new commandment: Love each other. Just as I have loved you, you should love each other. Your love for one another will prove to the world that you are my disciples." JOHN 13:34-35

DAY 228

☼ A prayer about RISKS
When I wonder what risks I should take

HEAVENLY FATHER,

Those who love me are always warning me about the risks of certain things, like getting distracted when I drive, walking across a busy street at night, or getting involved with friends who might influence me the wrong way. It's easy just to smile and nod at their comments because I don't think I'm very likely to get hurt from doing these things. But I know your Word warns me about risks too. Teach me to listen when you tell me to be careful not to let my anger control me, to be cautious around people who willfully go against your rules, to guard my heart and keep it from sin. Help me to realize that your warnings are there to protect me and keep me far from destructive situations. Show me, too, that you don't intend for me to be cautious all the time. You encourage me to take risks that result in a godly life—risks such as reaching out to someone else, going on a missions trip, or accepting a new challenge. I pray for the wisdom to know when I should step out in faith to follow your call. Thank you for being with me in this adventure of life!

Commit everything you do to the LORD. Trust him, and he will help you. PSALM 37:5

☼ A prayer about REPENTANCE
When I need to foster repentance

LORD,

I confess that sometimes I take your grace too lightly. I commit a sin, ask your forgiveness, and then commit the same sin again—only to ask your forgiveness again. You are gracious to forgive, but I know this pattern is not what you want for me. You want to free me from sin and transform me completely. Please soften my heart and bring me to true repentance. May I not only admit my sin but also commit to changing the direction of my life, with your help. Teach me that turning from my sin will allow me to experience your fullest blessings. I don't want sin to rule my life. May I decide wholeheartedly to move toward you instead of away from you. I know you will always guide me in the right direction.

Peter's words pierced their hearts, and they said to him and to the other apostles, "Brothers, what should we do?" Peter replied, "Each of you must repent of your sins and turn to God, and be baptized in the name of Jesus Christ for the forgiveness of your sins. Then you will receive the gift of the Holy Spirit." ACTS 2:37-38

☼ A prayer about LISTENING
When I want to listen more carefully to God

LORD GOD,

I know you speak to me, but often I am too busy to pay attention. I want to commit to spending quiet time with you each day. Teach me to be still before you and to wait expectantly. I know you will speak to me as I pray and meditate on your Word. Help me to stop all my talking and thinking and planning for a few minutes and rest in you. May my ears be open to what you want to tell me.

Each morning I bring my requests to you and wait expectantly.
PSALM 5:3

DAY 231 *Prayerful Moment*

☼ A prayer about WORSHIP
When I want to worship God

LORD JESUS,

You are to be honored above everything, and one day everyone will worship you. You are Lord! I praise you because you are almighty and all-knowing, yet you sacrificed yourself for me. May I worship you with a pure heart, because only you are worthy.

God elevated him to the place of highest honor and gave him the name above all other names, that at the name of Jesus every knee should bow, in heaven and on earth and under the earth, and every tongue confess that Jesus Christ is Lord, to the glory of God the Father. PHILIPPIANS 2:9-11

⚙ A prayer about TALKING TO GOD
When I wonder how I benefit from prayer

FATHER,

When I pray, I tend to get stuck in a rut. I thank you for food and ask you for help with some daily tasks—and that's about it. But I know there is so much more. You want to hear from me and speak to me. You want to show me more of yourself through prayer. Teach me, Lord, that when I listen to you, you can share your wisdom and resources with me. You can soften my heart and help me deal with negative emotions like anger, resentment, and bitterness. You can transform my thoughts and attitudes. You can increase my knowledge of you and my desire for you. Help me to be faithful in prayer! When my prayer life is becoming rote, remind me of these wonderful blessings you want to share with me through vibrant, living conversation with you.

Let us come boldly to the throne of our gracious God. There we will receive his mercy, and we will find grace to help us when we need it most. HEBREWS 4:16

DAY 233

☼ A prayer about STUBBORNNESS
When I need a softer heart

LORD,

I confess that too often I think I know what is best for me. I want to follow my plans and do things my way. I don't want to follow the rules for living that I find in the Bible, and I don't want to admit that your plans for me might actually be better than my own. Help me, Lord. Break through my stubbornness. Show me how to give up the things I think are so good and exchange them for things you know are so much better. Help me to trust that you love me and want what is best for me. May I be honest enough to look at my own decisions and realize that they're not really getting me that far in life. What do I have to lose if I stop being stubborn and humbly follow your path? Only my own pride. But I'll gain your approval, all the benefits that come from following you, and the relief that comes from no longer having to prove myself. Please soften my heart so I will always be responsive to you.

[The Lord says,] "I will give you a new heart, and I will put a new spirit in you. I will take out your stony, stubborn heart and give you a tender, responsive heart."
EZEKIEL 36:26

☀ **A prayer about WORK**
When I want to find meaning in work

FATHER,

Sometimes I think of work as just a way to get money. It is that, but it's also part of your plan for my life. It matters to you, and because of that, I want to take it seriously. Please help me see that I am actually working for you. The tasks I'm doing are important, but my motives are even more important. May my aim be to please you. Teach me that when I work faithfully, I will gain respect from my employer and will be a more credible witness to the unbelievers around me. Impress on my heart that you have put me in this position for a reason, and help me to do my work to the best of my ability. Then I will honor you every day.

Make it your goal to live a quiet life, minding your own business and working with your hands, just as we instructed you before. Then people who are not Christians will respect the way you live, and you will not need to depend on others.
I THESSALONIANS 4:11-12

☼ A prayer about NEGLECT
When I've been neglecting time with God

LORD,

I have not spent much time talking with you recently. I haven't been as faithful as I should be about going to church and meeting with other believers, and I haven't even read my Bible. I know I am neglecting you. Please help me to realize that this is harmful to me. When I drift away from you, I lose my passion for the faith, I fall into temptation more easily, I give up the encouragement and joy that can come from worship, and I miss out on the guidance in your Word. Forgive me, Lord. I don't want to drift away from the truth. Draw me near to you. Then give me the desire and the willpower to stay close always.

Let us hold tightly without wavering to the hope we affirm, for God can be trusted to keep his promise. Let us think of ways to motivate one another to acts of love and good works. And let us not neglect our meeting together, as some people do, but encourage one another, especially now that the day of his return is drawing near. HEBREWS 10:23-25

☼ A prayer about QUESTIONS
When I have questions about God's plan

LORD,

Is it okay to ask you questions? I don't always understand why things are happening the way they are or even how faith really works in my life. When I read your Word, I see other people who questioned you, like Moses, and you were patient with them. Thank you for being patient with me, too. Teach me that I don't really need to know all my future circumstances or the reasons behind your actions. What I really need is to know that you are with me. You are in control of all the details of my life, so I don't need to be. Show me that when I question my circumstances, you often respond by showing me more of your character so I can learn to love and trust you more. As I go through seasons of doubt in my life, I pray that asking the tough questions will always lead me right back to you.

One day Moses said to the LORD, "You have been telling me, 'Take these people up to the Promised Land.' But you haven't told me whom you will send with me. . . . Let me know your ways so I may understand you more fully and continue to enjoy your favor. . . ." The LORD replied, "I will personally go with you, Moses, and I will give you rest—everything will be fine for you." EXODUS 33:12-14

☼ A prayer about HOPE
When I am discouraged

GOD OF HOPE,

Everything seems to be falling apart right now. I'm holding tight to the fact that you keep your Word. You promise that in heaven all of my problems and suffering will be over. Never again will I grieve or be discouraged. May that hope for the future get me through my present struggles.

Lead me by your truth and teach me, for you are the God who saves me. All day long I put my hope in you. PSALM 25:5

DAY 238 *Prayerful Moment*

☼ A prayer about SUCCESS
When I want to be successful in God's eyes

HEAVENLY FATHER,

The people around me usually define *success* by how much a person owns and how much he or she achieves. Yet I don't think that's how you define it. Teach me that in your eyes, success is measured not by material assets but by spiritual ones, not by what I have but by who I am, not by what I know but by who I know. O Lord, help me to pursue spiritual maturity, godly character, and a close relationship with you. Then I will be successful in your sight.

Our goal is to please him. 2 CORINTHIANS 5:9

☼ **A prayer about RENEWAL**
When I am disappointed in myself

GRACIOUS LORD,

I have made some mistakes, and I'm so disappointed with myself. I have good intentions, but they never last. Life is so much messier than I expected! I find myself wishing I could start over. When I'm discouraged, teach me that renewal begins with your compassion and my willingness to change. I pray for a soft heart that is ready for the transformation that can come only from you. When I have it, I will find a new beginning. My soul will be refreshed and my heart revived. Thank you, Lord, that you promise to restore any heart that seeks a new start. Please forgive my sin and cleanse me completely. May I turn away from the sin that has brought me down and instead turn to you with a sincere desire for renewal.

Since you have heard about Jesus and have learned the truth that comes from him, throw off your old sinful nature and your former way of life, which is corrupted by lust and deception. Instead, let the Spirit renew your thoughts and attitudes. Put on your new nature, created to be like God—truly righteous and holy. EPHESIANS 4:21-24

☼ **A prayer about WORRY**
  When I am overwhelmed by worry

HEAVENLY FATHER,

When I worry too much, I get distracted. I feel frozen, and it becomes difficult to make wise decisions. My worries crowd out the good in my life and keep me focused on my problems, which only makes them seem worse. I need your help, Lord. Free me from my worry. Teach me that the key to finding rest is first to admit that I can't control the future and then to entrust myself to you, the one who holds the future in your hands. Help me to give my concerns to you. As I do, they will begin to seem smaller and smaller. Release me from this prison of worry and renew my hope, Lord. I know that I will find joy when I place my life in your hands.

[Jesus said,] "That is why I tell you not to worry about everyday life—whether you have enough food and drink, or enough clothes to wear. Isn't life more than food, and your body more than clothing? Look at the birds. They don't plant or harvest or store food in barns, for your heavenly Father feeds them. And aren't you far more valuable to him than they are? Can all your worries add a single moment to your life?" MATTHEW 6:25-27

☼ A prayer about PRESSURE
When I am facing pressure to do what is wrong

LORD,

My friends are putting a lot of pressure on me to do things that I know are wrong. It's hard to deal with. I don't want to alienate my friends, but I want to make the right choices. Please give me wisdom. Show me the right course of action. Maybe I need to remove myself from the situation entirely—or even stop hanging around with those friends for a while. Please give me the courage I need to walk away, if that's what I need to do to keep myself out of trouble. Teach me to pay attention to that heavy feeling in my heart when I'm about to make a choice that I'll regret. I know that's your way of getting my attention before the pressure becomes too much for me to handle. Help me to take that way of escape when you provide it. I want to do what's right, Lord. Thank you that you want me to succeed too, and that you are with me every step of the way.

Oh, the joys of those who do not follow the advice of the wicked, or stand around with sinners, or join in with mockers. But they delight in the law of the LORD, meditating on it day and night. They are like trees planted along the riverbank, bearing fruit each season. Their leaves never wither, and they prosper in all they do. PSALM 1:1-3

☀ **A prayer about PROMISES**
   When I am facing doubts

LOVING GOD,

Sometimes I struggle with doubt. I wonder if you really are who you say you are, and if you can really do what you say you will. Yet I know that your words are totally reliable. You are the author of truth! Draw me to your Word to learn more about your promises, which are given to me and to all believers. I want to grow in my faith, Lord. I want to trust you more and get rid of my doubts. Please meet me as I study your promises. May they remind me of how deeply you love me and how much you want to have a relationship with me. May I discover more and more about your character and the wonderful things in my future. Teach me that your promises are the rock-solid foundation on which I can build my faith.

No, I will not break my covenant; I will not take back a single word I said. . . . In my holiness I cannot lie.
PSALM 89:34-35

DAY 243

❂ A prayer about CONVICTION
When the Holy Spirit is working in my heart

LORD,

I sense your Holy Spirit at work in my life, telling me what is right and wrong. He is convicting me, showing me places where I have compromised or fallen away from your truth. Thank you for the gift of the Holy Spirit. Without his conviction, I would be unprepared to face temptation and would easily give in when my faith is challenged. I need you to hold me steady on the path of life. Help me to live out and act on my faith in practical ways. Keep my convictions sharp as I read your Word. May my heart remain soft so that I will always respond to your gentle leading.

Let the Holy Spirit guide your lives. Then you won't be doing what your sinful nature craves. The sinful nature wants to do evil, which is just the opposite of what the Spirit wants. And the Spirit gives us desires that are the opposite of what the sinful nature desires. . . . The Holy Spirit produces this kind of fruit in our lives: love, joy, peace, patience, kindness, goodness, faithfulness, gentleness, and self-control.
GALATIANS 5:16-17, 22-23

✺ **A prayer about SERVING**
   *When I wonder how serving others shows my love
   for God*

LORD OF LOVE,
Your Word teaches that love is an action. Love is doing something for another person with no thought of getting anything in return. Teach me that kind of love, Lord. Please help me to demonstrate my love through acts of kindness and service. I want to give of myself for others' well-being. You have done so much for me. May I respond in gratitude by sharing your love with those around me.

He will not forget . . . how you have shown your love to him by caring for other believers. HEBREWS 6:10

✺ **A prayer about HELPLESSNESS**
   When I am powerless

FATHER,
I come to you today in desperate need. I am struggling, downcast, and completely helpless. I need you! When I try to get myself out of trouble, I miss out on seeing what you can do in my life. You are the one who loves doing the impossible. I reach out to you, my lifeline, and trust that you will help me.

Asa cried out to the LORD his God, "O LORD, no one but you can help the powerless against the mighty! Help us, O LORD our God, for we trust in you alone." 2 CHRONICLES 14:11

☼ A prayer about PERSPECTIVE
When my perspective is too limited

LORD OF THE FUTURE,

From my perspective, the world often seems to be random and unpredictable. I don't see much rhyme or reason to why some people thrive and others struggle. Help me to remember that my human perspective is so limited. You are in control, even if I can't see it now. When I read in your Word about Joseph, I'm reminded that you used even his brothers' terrible actions to fulfill your own plan. They sinned in treating Joseph cruelly, yet their sin did not thwart your purposes. You are sovereign. Teach me that what I can see now is like the back of a tapestry—full of knots and loose ends. But someday I will see the front of the tapestry in its beautiful entirety. When I can look from your perspective, I'll see how you have shaped world history as well as the details of my own life. Even in unexpected circumstances, may I be able to embrace both the good and the bad because I trust that you are weaving a beautiful picture with my life.

Now we see things imperfectly, like puzzling reflections in a mirror, but then we will see everything with perfect clarity. All that I know now is partial and incomplete, but then I will know everything completely, just as God now knows me completely. I CORINTHIANS 13:12

☀ **A prayer about WORTH**
When I wonder how valuable I am to God

LORD,

I tend to base my self-worth on a combination of my accomplishments, credentials, appearance, possessions, or social status. Yet I know that's a precarious foundation. If I let my efforts slip, have a bad day at work, lose my newest possession, or find out that my friends have turned on me, my opinion of myself falls. Teach me to find my self-worth in my relationship with you. Only that is secure and lasting. Thank you for valuing me! Your Word tells me that you created me and knew me intimately even before I was born. You loved me enough to rescue me from sin. I am awed to know that I have great worth in your eyes. May this assurance free me from comparing myself to others or competing for status. Instead, let me rest in your unchanging love for me.

Even before he made the world, God loved us and chose us in Christ to be holy and without fault in his eyes. God decided in advance to adopt us into his own family by bringing us to himself through Jesus Christ. This is what he wanted to do, and it gave him great pleasure. So we praise God for the glorious grace he has poured out on us who belong to his dear Son. He is so rich in kindness and grace that he purchased our freedom with the blood of his Son and forgave our sins.
EPHESIANS 1:4-7

☼ A prayer about REACHING OUT
When I want to help those less fortunate

FATHER,

I'm grateful for the passages in your Word that challenge believers to care about the poor and needy. Your compassion is so evident in all the laws that made provision for those who couldn't care for themselves. I pray that you will grow that same compassion in me. It's tempting to justify my lack of care by thinking that poor people are somehow at fault for their circumstances. But while that may occasionally be true, the truth is that there are many people around me who legitimately need help. Teach me that feeling sorry for people is not enough; I need to act on my compassion. May I look for tangible ways to help others with my time or money. I always want to remember that helping others is not just an obligation. It's a privilege that will bring great joy.

Feed the hungry, and help those in trouble. Then your light will shine out from the darkness, and the darkness around you will be as bright as noon. The LORD will guide you continually, giving you water when you are dry and restoring your strength. ISAIAH 58:10-11

☼ A prayer about COURAGE
When life is frightening

LORD,

This world can be a scary place. At times I will face stress, major illness, difficulties with money, hurtful relationships, and even danger. When I'm afraid, help me to turn to you. I know that courage isn't about pretending to be brave or ignoring the danger. Instead, it comes from knowing that you are stronger than my biggest problem or my worst enemy. Nothing is too big for you to handle! When I face a threat, I do not face it alone. You are always with me, defending me. Thank you, Lord. May I never forget that the source of my courage isn't my own strength but your strength. With you, I can be confident. When I concentrate on your presence with me, I can build up the courage I need to go on and face whatever lies ahead.

Don't be afraid, for I am with you. Don't be discouraged, for I am your God. I will strengthen you and help you. I will hold you up with my victorious right hand. ISAIAH 41:10

☼ **A prayer about AMBITION**
When I wonder what my highest ambitions should be

LORD,

I have such a desire to do something important and worthwhile. Yet I want to be sure my motives aren't selfish. What can I pursue that won't really be about trying to get recognition for myself? Help me to remember that having a vital relationship with you is something I can always pursue without reservation. May that be my highest ambition. Teach me also that goals that benefit other people are also worth pursuing. Give me a heart that desires to bring justice, peace, and your love to the world. May I hunger and thirst to show mercy, to share your redeeming love with others, and to expand your Kingdom by caring for others as you care for them. These are ambitions that will please you.

God blesses those who hunger and thirst for justice, for they will be satisfied. God blesses those who are merciful, for they will be shown mercy. God blesses those whose hearts are pure, for they will see God. God blesses those who work for peace, for they will be called the children of God.
MATTHEW 5:6-9

☼ A prayer about USEFULNESS
When I want God to use me

ALMIGHTY GOD,

You are strong and I am weak—yet sometimes I make the mistake of relying on my own power. Teach me to trust in you rather than in myself. When I acknowledge my need for your Holy Spirit, your power can flow through me, just as electric current flows through a wire. May I be a conduit of your power to the world around me.

All glory to God, who is able, through his mighty power at work within us, to accomplish infinitely more than we might ask or think. EPHESIANS 3:20

DAY 252 *Prayerful Moment*

☼ A prayer about SACRIFICE
When I am amazed by Jesus' sacrifice

LORD JESUS,

You gave your very life so that I could live forever. When I think about your great sacrifice, I am amazed and humbled. I will never be worthy of it, and you don't ask me to be. But I do want to be grateful. May my heart overflow with thanksgiving, Lord. Keep me from ever taking your sacrifice lightly.

He is Jesus Christ, the one who is truly righteous. He himself is the sacrifice that atones for our sins—and not only our sins but the sins of all the world. 1 JOHN 2:1-2

DAY 253

☀ **A prayer about APPROVAL**
When I wonder how I can gain God's approval

FATHER GOD,

When others don't like the way I look or the words I say, I feel their disapproval, and that doesn't always seem fair. When I live in a way that goes against your Word's commands for life, I sense your disapproval too. I don't like how that feels, but I know it's fair because your opinion is not subjective. Yet I can never measure up to your perfect standard, so sometimes I get discouraged. How can I ever gain your approval? Help me remember that I am your child. Your Word tells me that you love and accept me not for what I do but for who I am. You created me and gave me worth. You love me and approve of me because I am yours. That will never change, no matter what others think of me. I praise you for loving me eternally. Nothing I can do will cause you to love me less. May that motivate me to do all I can to please you—not out of fear, but out of love and gratitude.

No power in the sky above or in the earth below—indeed, nothing in all creation will ever be able to separate us from the love of God that is revealed in Christ Jesus our Lord.
ROMANS 8:39

☀ **A prayer about MYSTERY**
When I can't understand everything about God

LORD GOD,

Your nature and knowledge are beyond my understanding. If that weren't true, you wouldn't be God. I long to know you, and you have promised that I can know you enough to be in a relationship with you. But let me never forget that your ways are far above mine. I will never fully understand you because I can never be equal to you. Teach me that your mysteries are opportunities for my faith. If I knew everything there was to know about you, I wouldn't need to trust you. Help me to remember, Lord, that you have given me everything I need to know to believe in you and obey you. Yet you allow me to increase my knowledge as I study your Word and walk with you. Thank you that following you is a lifelong adventure of discovery. And thank you that one day in heaven, I will see you as you really are. Your glory will be fully revealed, and it will be an amazing moment!

Dear friends, we are already God's children, but he has not yet shown us what we will be like when Christ appears. But we do know that we will be like him, for we will see him as he really is. 1 JOHN 3:2

☀ A prayer about ASSERTIVENESS
When I'm not sure if it's okay to be assertive

LORD JESUS,

Sometimes I think the Christian way to act is to be quiet, not rock the boat, and above all, be "nice." But that doesn't really describe the way you acted when you were on earth. You were often assertive when you spoke to the Pharisees and other religious leaders, because you were trying to show them how wrong some of their practices were. Teach me that being assertive doesn't mean being unkind or angry—it just means standing up for what is right or making my concerns known. Please give me the wisdom to know when I need to take a stand, and the courage to do it. I want to do what is right. May my assertiveness be informed by truth and tempered with love.

O people, the LORD has told you what is good, and this is what he requires of you: to do what is right, to love mercy, and to walk humbly with your God. MICAH 6:8

☼ A prayer about DISCOURAGEMENT
When I can't see beyond my problems

LORD,

When I'm discouraged, I tend to focus only on my own problems. I lose all perspective, and I forget that you are near and ready to help. That's what happened to the people of Judah when they saw the vast enemy army gathering to attack their city but didn't see you standing by to protect them. They were so afraid and discouraged that they couldn't even see their own salvation! Please give me eyes to see your presence in my life. May I never let my feelings of discouragement shake my assurance of your love for me. Discouragement can make me doubt your love, but that only pulls me away from my greatest source of help. I know you are working in my life. Even when I can't see what you're doing, help me to believe that you will fight on my behalf. You will help me succeed as I trust in you.

This is what the LORD says: Do not be afraid! Don't be discouraged by this mighty army, for the battle is not yours, but God's. . . . You will not even need to fight. Take your positions; then stand still and watch the LORD's victory. He is with you, O people of Judah and Jerusalem. Do not be afraid or discouraged. 2 CHRONICLES 20:15, 17

☀ **A prayer about SALVATION**
*When I wonder how eternal salvation should affect
my life now*

LORD,

I know that the wonderful inheritance you have promised me in the future should change my life now, in the present. You have offered me the free gift of salvation, with eternal life in heaven. My future is guaranteed! This frees me to take part in the plan you have for me. I can be confident that nothing can harm my soul or endanger my eternal future. I am secure in you. Teach me that I can take risks by stepping out in faith when you are asking me to do something for you. I can be generous, knowing you care for me. O Lord, your gift of salvation is so immense. Help me to live as though my future holds everything I could ever want—because it truly does.

We know that our old sinful selves were crucified with Christ so that sin might lose its power in our lives. We are no longer slaves to sin. For when we died with Christ we were set free from the power of sin. And since we died with Christ, we know we will also live with him. ROMANS 6:6-8

⚙ **A prayer about THANKFULNESS**
   When I want to become more thankful

LORD GOD,

I want to have a thankful heart. I know the best way to cultivate thankfulness is simply by giving thanks regularly. Help me to set aside time every day for gratitude. No matter what my feelings are, may I make a mental list of all of your blessings and thank you for them. As giving thanks becomes second nature, may I begin to see my struggles in the right perspective.

Be thankful in all circumstances, for this is God's will for you who belong to Christ Jesus. 1 THESSALONIANS 5:18

DAY 259 *Prayerful Moment*

⚙ **A prayer about ABILITIES**
   When I want to make the most of my gifts

HEAVENLY FATHER,

I know that you have given all people special abilities and spiritual gifts—even me! Please help me to identify them. I want to develop them and figure out the unique ways I can use them for your Kingdom and your glory.

My life is worth nothing to me unless I use it for finishing the work assigned me by the Lord Jesus. ACTS 20:24

DAY 260

☼ A prayer about REJECTION
When I worry that God might reject me

LORD,

Sometimes I am afraid that you might reject me if I commit a really terrible sin or even if I go too many days without reading the Bible. But when I feel that way, all I have to do is look at the reassuring passages in your Word. You have promised that you will accept everyone who comes to you in faith. You understand my weaknesses, yet you encourage me to approach you boldly and receive your mercy. You don't stand around waiting for me to fail at this life of faith. You want me to succeed—to draw near to you and be forgiven, to experience your love and grace, to live full of purpose. Thank you that you will never reject me or send me away, but you welcome me with love.

This High Priest of ours understands our weaknesses, for he faced all of the same testings we do, yet he did not sin. So let us come boldly to the throne of our gracious God. There we will receive his mercy, and we will find grace to help us when we need it most. HEBREWS 4:15-16

☼ A prayer about FINISHING WELL
When I need to persevere to the end

O GOD,

I have great intentions in so many areas of my life, but often I don't follow through. Then I'm doubly disappointed, because not only have I missed out on the reward I'd hoped for, but I have to face the fact that I've wasted my time and effort. I want to finish what I start. Teach me to develop a clear picture of my end goal. I know that when I see clearly where I am going and what my good intentions can accomplish, I will be more motivated to follow through. If my intention is to send an encouraging note to a friend, I could picture my friend receiving it and being uplifted. If my intention is to study your Word and get to know you better, I could picture myself reading the Bible with a smile on my face, encouraged and strengthened. Help me to set the right goals, Lord. When I try to do too many things, I end up finishing none of them. Direct me to the priorities I should have or the changes I need to make in my life right now. Then guide me as I set goals, work hard, and commit to finishing well.

Finishing is better than starting. Patience is better than pride. ECCLESIASTES 7:8

☼ A prayer about SILENCE
When I feel as if God is silent

LORD,

I don't see you working in my life right now, and I'm struggling to hear your voice. I know you're there, so why can't I hear you? Please give me wisdom as I try to discern the reason. Teach me that sometimes you are silent because you're waiting for me to do something—to turn away from a sinful habit, to follow a call that you have made clear, or just to stop and listen to you. Forgive me for times when I persist in sin. I know that when I do that, I'm choosing to move further away from you, and that will make it harder for me to hear your voice. Teach me also that sometimes what seems like silence to me is really just you answering my prayers with "no" or "wait." Give me the maturity to realize that I can't expect you to do exactly what I want; instead, I need to get in line with your plans. Keep me from assuming that you're not acting just because you don't answer my prayers the way I'd like. Even if I don't know why you seem silent, may I never give up my faith that you are with me and your love will never fail.

As for me, I look to the LORD for help. I wait confidently for God to save me, and my God will certainly hear me.
MICAH 7:7

☼ A prayer about CHOICES
When I want to make better choices

LORD JESUS,

When I read the story of Zacchaeus in your Word, I'm struck by the bad choices he'd made. He made his living by cheating people out of money they couldn't afford to lose. Some even called him a "notorious sinner"! Yet after you spent some time with him, Zacchaeus was changed, and he wanted to make better choices. As I spend time with you, Lord Jesus, may my heart become aligned with yours. My choices reflect the kind of person I am, and I want to be first and foremost a follower of you. Soften my heart so that I will not stay the same, but will be changed by your influence and will make choices that please you. Help me to remember that Zacchaeus's best choice was to welcome an encounter with you in the first place. May I always welcome your transforming power in my life!

"Zacchaeus!" [Jesus] said. "Quick, come down! I must be a guest in your home today." Zacchaeus quickly climbed down and took Jesus to his house in great excitement and joy. But the people were displeased. "He has gone to be the guest of a notorious sinner," they grumbled. Meanwhile, Zacchaeus stood before the Lord and said, "I will give half my wealth to the poor, Lord, and if I have cheated people on their taxes, I will give them back four times as much!" LUKE 19:5-8

☼ A prayer about PERSECUTION
When I wonder why Christians have to endure persecution

LORD GOD,

One of the hardest things for me to deal with is being scorned, mocked, or ignored by others because of my faith in you. I'm not ashamed of you, but sometimes I just want to fit in. Yet I know that these hard times will help my character to grow. Teach me that the way I handle persecution shows who I really am on the inside. Please give me the grace to endure it, that I may show you and those around me that my commitment to you is real. May I look at each trial as an opportunity for my faith to become strong and genuine. Please provide the strength I need to endure whatever comes so that I may make an impact for eternity. And Lord, help me also to remember those who are being more severely persecuted for their faith—my brothers and sisters around the world who are being tortured or imprisoned or are even dying because they follow you.

We can rejoice, too, when we run into problems and trials, for we know that they help us develop endurance. And endurance develops strength of character, and character strengthens our confident hope of salvation. And this hope will not lead to disappointment. For we know how dearly God loves us, because he has given us the Holy Spirit to fill our hearts with his love. ROMANS 5:3-5

☯ **A prayer about LOVE**
When I want to love others

LORD,

I usually associate *love* with romantic feelings. But your Word makes clear that love is more than an emotion. It's also a commitment. Teach me that my ability to love does not depend on my warm feelings. Instead, it comes from a decision to consistently extend myself for someone else's well-being. I want to love others the way you love me. I trust that you will help me.

[Jesus said,] "Your love for one another will prove to the world that you are my disciples." JOHN 13:35

DAY 266 *Prayerful Moment*

☯ **A prayer about THE ARTS**
When I want to praise God through the arts

CREATOR GOD,

You have made me creative. I thank you that I can express myself in artistic ways—through worshiping, singing, loving, helping, playing music, painting, creating beautiful objects, writing, or even thinking through problems. Humans are creative because you are creative—in fact, you are the Creator of all. Help me to honor you through my creativity. Thank you for the times when you touch my heart and emotions through the arts.

Sing a new song of praise to him; play skillfully on the harp, and sing with joy. PSALM 33:3

☼ A prayer about SHARING
When I want to be more generous

LORD,

My parents have been trying to teach me about sharing since I was in preschool! You'd think it would have sunk in by now, but it's still almost as hard as ever to share my things, my time, and myself. I know it's because at my very core I desire to get instead of give, to accumulate instead of relinquish, to look out for myself instead of caring for others. I confess my selfish attitude, Lord. I know you have called me to share many things—my money, my faith, my love, my time, my talents. Impress on my heart how much you have shared with me. How can I hold tightly to the temporary things of this world when you have given your very life for my salvation? Ignite in me a spirit of greater generosity. May I develop a heart that loves to share freely with others because I know how much I already have.

May you be filled with joy, always thanking the Father. He has enabled you to share in the inheritance that belongs to his people, who live in the light. COLOSSIANS 1:11-12

☀ A prayer about DETERMINATION
When I need greater resolve for spiritual battle

MIGHTY GOD,

Your Word is clear that I need to be on the alert for Satan's attacks, yet too often I lack the sense of urgency that would give me greater resolve. Renew my determination, Lord. I want to do my best for you, and that means not getting tripped up by temptation. Teach me to have confidence in you, recognizing that you are mightier than Satan and will one day defeat him. Nudge me to call on you in prayer, asking you to fill me with the knowledge of your Spirit. Help me to study your Word with focus, claim your promises of victory, and realize the blessings that will come when Satan is defeated forever. May I have the courage and confidence to persevere in my fight because I know that you promise ultimate victory to all who believe in you and obey you.

Be strong in the Lord and in his mighty power. Put on all of God's armor so that you will be able to stand firm against all strategies of the devil. For we are not fighting against flesh-and-blood enemies, but against evil rulers and authorities of the unseen world, against mighty powers in this dark world, and against evil spirits in the heavenly places. Therefore, put on every piece of God's armor so you will be able to resist the enemy in the time of evil. Then after the battle you will still be standing firm. EPHESIANS 6:10-13

☼ A prayer about TIME
   When I want to make good use of my time

LORD,

I'm young, and my life is stretched out before me. I feel as if I have so much time to accomplish whatever I want to do. Yet the truth is that none of us knows exactly how much time we have left on this earth. It's not your will for me to live in fear of what might happen, but at the same time you tell me to be wise, making the most of every opportunity. Teach me that time is valuable. Challenge me to use it purposefully for things that count, not waste it on things that are meaningless. Help me to be wise and thoughtful about my time, never taking it for granted.

"LORD, remind me how brief my time on earth will be. Remind me that my days are numbered—how fleeting my life is. You have made my life no longer than the width of my hand. My entire lifetime is just a moment to you; at best, each of us is but a breath." . . . *And so, Lord, where do I put my hope? My only hope is in you.* PSALM 39:4-5, 7

☼ A prayer about SUFFERING
   When I wonder why people have to suffer

MERCIFUL LORD,

Why is there so much suffering in the world? And why do some people seem to suffer so much more than others? Some suffering, like losing someone to cancer or a car accident, seems to happen because of the random effects of this fallen world. Other suffering happens because of neglect, such as when I fall behind in my responsibilities and I struggle because I wasted time surfing the Internet. And I know some suffering comes because of sin; if I deliberately go against your commands, I may suffer the consequences. O Lord, help me to be wise so that I can avoid bringing unnecessary suffering on myself. Yet teach me to accept that some suffering comes to everyone, no matter how godly. I may never understand all the reasons for suffering, but I can grasp the fact that you are present in my hurt. Thank you for comforting me in my sorrow. May my suffering prepare me to comfort someone else who is hurting.

The LORD is close to the brokenhearted; he rescues those whose spirits are crushed. PSALM 34:18

DAY 271

✸ A prayer about KNOWING GOD
When I wonder what it means to know God

LORD GOD,

You are the Creator of all and high above all. It's amazing that you care about humans at all, let alone that you want to have a relationship with each of us individually. Thank you for knowing me and loving me! Thank you for the gift of prayer, which allows me to communicate with you. I'm grateful that you want to talk with me, yet sometimes I wonder how this can ever work since you are so great and I am so small. How can I ever understand who you are or what you are saying to me? But I'm comforted by the promise in your Word that those who believe in you have the mind of Christ. You have provided your Holy Spirit to help me understand you and your ways. Thank you that he gives guidance, wisdom, and discernment. Teach me to listen and learn.

"Who can know the LORD's thoughts? Who knows enough to teach him?" But we understand these things, for we have the mind of Christ. 1 CORINTHIANS 2:16

DAY 272 *Prayerful Moment*

☼ A prayer about PRAISE
When I want to celebrate your goodness

ALMIGHTY GOD,

I am full of praise today. I am so thankful for what you have done for me that I want to tell everyone I meet! You are great, O Lord—so great I can't even begin to comprehend it. May my heart always overflow with praise. As I worship you, may I rejoice in the knowledge that you are my God.

Give thanks to the LORD and proclaim his greatness. Let the whole world know what he has done. Sing to him; yes, sing his praises. Tell everyone about his wonderful deeds.
PSALM 105:1-2

DAY 273 *Prayerful Moment*

☼ A prayer about THE HOLY SPIRIT
When I am amazed by the Holy Spirit

LORD,

I'm amazed when I remember that your Holy Spirit lives in me. He is dwelling within me, helping me understand the truth about salvation and discover the mysteries of your character. Thank you for providing a way to help me distinguish between right and wrong and to convict me when I sin. May I never take this wonderful gift for granted.

We have received God's Spirit (not the world's spirit), so we can know the wonderful things God has freely given us.
1 CORINTHIANS 2:12

DAY 274

☼ **A prayer about BEING OVERWHELMED**
When I am facing big obstacles

LORD GOD,

I'm facing an overwhelming obstacle right now, one that seems impossible to overcome. The task is too big, the challenges too great, my emotions too strained. I am exhausted. Teach me to take one day at a time. May I be faithful now, in this moment. When I don't have the energy or even the faith to look toward the big goal, help me to focus on today's tasks. You know my weaknesses, Lord, and I trust you to help me. I know that when I am weak, you are strong. You can accomplish the task if I just do my part. When I'm frightened by hardships and obstacles, please help me to recognize them as the things that will actually strengthen my faith. As I take one step at a time in obedience to you, I trust you to help me overcome the obstacles and reach the goal.

[Paul said,] "I was given a thorn in my flesh. . . . Three times I begged the Lord to take it away. Each time he said, 'My grace is all you need. My power works best in weakness.' So now I am glad to boast about my weaknesses, so that the power of Christ can work through me. That's why I take pleasure in my weaknesses, and in the insults, hardships, persecutions, and troubles that I suffer for Christ. For when I am weak, then I am strong."
2 CORINTHIANS 12:7-10

☼ A prayer about JOY
When I wonder how I can find lasting joy

LORD GOD,

My feelings rise and fall—sometimes I'm positive and excited, and sometimes I'm discouraged. That's just a part of life, because you created me to have emotions. But I also want something that runs much deeper than my momentary feelings. I want to experience lasting joy and contentment. Teach me, Lord, that if my feelings are like the stormy surface of an ocean, my joy can be like a strong current that runs far underneath. Joy comes from walking closely with you and knowing that your love for me is too great to measure. Not only that, you are almighty God! Nothing is too hard for you. I am secure in your hands, and that gives me joy, no matter what my emotions or my circumstances.

I have learned how to be content with whatever I have. I know how to live on almost nothing or with everything. I have learned the secret of living in every situation, whether it is with a full stomach or empty, with plenty or little.
PHILIPPIANS 4:11-12

☀ A prayer about PLEASURE
When I am caught up in pursuing pleasure

HEAVENLY FATHER,

My culture tells me that pleasure should be one of my main goals in life. And it's easy for me to get caught up in pursuing things that look good, feel good, and entertain me. Yet when that's my focus, I end up feeling empty. The more I pursue pleasure, the more I need. It's never-ending and eventually exhausting. That's what King Solomon discovered—and he even got to the point of feeling that everything in life was meaningless. Protect me from reaching that extreme, Lord. Teach me that focusing on you and on others will renew my attitude and give new meaning to my life. When I'm always thinking of myself, life seems dull and purposeless, and I lose my taste for things that are significant. But when I look to you, my sense of perspective is restored. Then I am able to enjoy pleasure in its rightful place.

I said to myself, "Come on, let's try pleasure. Let's look for the 'good things' in life." But I found that this, too, was meaningless. So I said, "Laughter is silly. What good does it do to seek pleasure?" After much thought, I decided to cheer myself with wine. . . . As I looked at everything I had worked so hard to accomplish, it was all so meaningless— like chasing the wind. There was nothing really worthwhile anywhere. ECCLESIASTES 2:1-3, 11

☼ A prayer about MY WITNESS
When I feel embarrassed to share my faith

LORD,

Sometimes I am teased or even ridiculed because of my faith in you. I want to fit in with the people around me, and I get embarrassed when others see how different I am. But I don't want to be ashamed of your Good News. Help me to remember that it really is good news! My belief in you is not about judging others or telling them they're wrong. Instead, it's about sharing your wonderful love and forgiveness that have changed my life. May I never forget that faith is a life-and-death matter. It's the most important thing there is. Give me courage, Lord. I need your strength to help me stand up for what I believe and share my faith with others. May I take your promises so seriously and be so filled with your joy and peace that those around me will become curious about my faith—and maybe even realize their own need for you.

I am not ashamed of this Good News about Christ. It is the power of God at work, saving everyone who believes.
ROMANS 1:16

⚙ A prayer about COMPETITION
When I wonder if it's okay to be competitive

LORD,

I like competition. Sometimes I thrive on the adrenaline of trying to get something done faster or better than someone else, or of beating my old record. Is that okay? I'm afraid that being competitive sometimes causes me to focus too much on pursuing my own goals instead of following your plans for me. If I'm caught up in my own efforts, I might forget about needing your help and trying to meet goals that benefit your Kingdom. I don't want to be like the people who built the Tower of Babel, so focused on celebrating my own accomplishments that I'm blind to the fact that those accomplishments don't do anything but make me feel important. Help me to remember that only the things done for your Kingdom have lasting value. Teach me, Lord, to channel my competitive nature into pursuing actions and accomplishments that will last for eternity.

They said, "Come, let's build a great city for ourselves with a tower that reaches into the sky. This will make us famous and keep us from being scattered all over the world." But the LORD . . . scattered them all over the world, and they stopped building the city. GENESIS 11:4-5, 8

⚙ **A prayer about SPIRITUAL ATTACK**
When I feel discouraged

FATHER,

I know that when I am most discouraged, I am most vulnerable to spiritual attack. Hold me close to you. Encourage me through your Word. Help me to cling to your promises that you are always with me, you are fighting for me, and you have the ultimate victory over Satan. Thank you for providing moments of comfort and encouragement just when I need them most.

Be strong and courageous! Do not be afraid or discouraged.
For the LORD your God is with you wherever you go.
JOSHUA 1:9

DAY 280 *Prayerful Moment*

⚙ **A prayer about REPUTATION**
When I want to have a good reputation

LORD,

I know that other people are forming opinions of me and my character based on what I do and say. Teach me to guard my reputation carefully. I want to be known for the right reasons—my integrity, kindness, and hard work—not the wrong ones. Help me to remember that when I live in obedience to you, I'll end up with a reputation that's above reproach.

Choose a good reputation over great riches; being held in
high esteem is better than silver or gold. PROVERBS 22:1

☼ **A prayer about LOVE**
When I wonder what it means to love God

LORD JESUS,

I need only to look at you to find a perfect example of unconditional love. You made the loving commitment to lay down your life to save me from my sin. Thank you! I want to love you with all my heart, soul, and strength, and I know one of the best ways to do that is to obey your commands. I can also show my love by resting in your words and pursuing the things you say are valuable. Teach me that when I make these kinds of choices, I am making a commitment to develop a relationship with you, the Creator of the universe. You loved me first, and you daily pursue me with your love. How can I not love you back?

The LORD says, "I will rescue those who love me. I will protect those who trust in my name. When they call on me, I will answer; I will be with them in trouble. I will rescue and honor them. I will reward them with a long life and give them my salvation." PSALM 91:14-16

☼ A prayer about PROMISES
When I wonder how God's promises affect my life

TRUSTWORTHY LORD,

When you seem far away or even irrelevant to my day-to-day life, teach me to remember your promises. Your Word is full of wonderful promises that have meaning not just for eternity, but now, every day of my life. You promise to be with me always, to forgive my sins, to carry my burdens, to give me peace of mind and heart, and to give me rest. Thank you, Lord! With you by my side, I don't need to be afraid. With you forgiving my sins, I can be free from my guilt. With you carrying my burdens, I am free from worry and anxiety. With you giving me rest, I don't have to exhaust myself by trying to prove I'm worthwhile. May I hold on to these promises every day. I'm so thankful for your faithfulness to me!

O LORD, God of Israel, there is no God like you in all of heaven above or on the earth below. You keep your covenant and show unfailing love to all who walk before you in wholehearted devotion. 1 KINGS 8:23

☼ **A prayer about THE HOLY SPIRIT**
   When I can't find words to pray

HEAVENLY FATHER,

When I am at my lowest point, I'm grateful that the Holy Spirit helps me pray. Sometimes I'm so full of grief, anger, or despair that I can't even form a coherent sentence. I long for someone to acknowledge my pain and understand what I am feeling, but I can't find the words. Thank you for promising in your Word that you hear and understand my prayers. Your Holy Spirit knows my deepest pain and longings—even when I can't sort them out myself. It's such a gift to be seen, to be known, to be heard, and to be comforted.

The Holy Spirit helps us in our weakness. For example, we don't know what God wants us to pray for. But the Holy Spirit prays for us with groanings that cannot be expressed in words. And the Father who knows all hearts knows what the Spirit is saying, for the Spirit pleads for us believers in harmony with God's own will. ROMANS 8:26-27

☀ A prayer about **PRIORITIES**
When I want to set the right priorities

HEAVENLY FATHER,

My life seems to skip from one interruption to another. I focus on what seems urgent at any given moment, but in the process I often miss what's really important. Teach me what matters most in life. I want to have the right priorities, and I want to set them now while I am young. Help me to put you first in my life. That seems difficult when I'm faced with deadlines and obligations. I don't want to disappoint anyone, and I want to do what's expected of me. But I know that if I make you my top priority, you will help me gain the right perspective on the rest of my life. You will show me what is worth being concerned about and what is not worth my time and energy. Oh Lord, teach me to seek you first—then everything else will fall into place.

Seek the Kingdom of God above all else, and live righteously, and he will give you everything you need. MATTHEW 6:33

DAY 285

⚙ **A prayer about MERCY**
When I am amazed by God's mercy

MERCIFUL GOD,

You shower amazing kindness on me, even though I don't deserve it. You offer me salvation and eternal life even though at times I have ignored you, neglected you, and rebelled against you. Your mercy sets me free from the power of sin. I am free to choose each day whether I will let my sinful nature control me, or whether I will allow your Holy Spirit to control me. Thank you, God, for your mercy that changes my life by showing me what it feels like to be loved, even though I have not always shown love in return. May I show this same mercy to others, and may they turn to you and receive it for themselves.

The LORD is compassionate and merciful, slow to get angry and filled with unfailing love. He will not constantly accuse us, nor remain angry forever. He does not punish us for all our sins; he does not deal harshly with us, as we deserve. For his unfailing love toward those who fear him is as great as the height of the heavens above the earth. He has removed our sins as far from us as the east is from the west.
PSALM 103:8-12

⚜ **A prayer about FEAR**
   When I am debilitated by fear

LORD,

Right now I feel paralyzed by fear, and it's distorting my view of reality. The problems in my path seem huge and overwhelming. Help me to remember that no matter how big they seem, they can never be more powerful than you. When I am afraid, may I never forget that you are with me, holding me by the hand. Then my fear will begin to recede.

For I hold you by your right hand—I, the LORD your God. And I say to you, "Don't be afraid. I am here to help you."
ISAIAH 41:13

DAY 287 *Prayerful Moment*

⚜ **A prayer about NATURE**
   When I am thankful for the beauties of creation

LORD,

Thank you for the wonderful inspiration of nature. You have created the world with such immense variety and breathtaking beauty. When I look at the natural world around me, I'm amazed at your creativity and the care you lavish on everything you have made. Thank you for creating this beauty for me to enjoy.

The heavens proclaim the glory of God. The skies display his craftsmanship. Day after day they continue to speak; night after night they make him known. PSALM 19:1-2

☀ A prayer about CELEBRATION
When I wonder what God thinks about fun

LORD,

Is it okay to have fun? Sometimes it seems like the Bible only talks about serious things. But when I look at the Old Testament more closely, I read about all the feasts and festivals you created for the Israelites. You came up with lots of opportunities for them to celebrate and enjoy life! Thank you that following you doesn't exclude fun. I'm grateful for joy and celebration, which lift my spirits and help me see beauty and meaning in life. I know these are only small tastes of the great joy I'll experience someday in heaven.

Nehemiah continued, "Go and celebrate with a feast of rich foods and sweet drinks, and share gifts of food with people who have nothing prepared. This is a sacred day before our Lord. Don't be dejected and sad, for the joy of the LORD is your strength!" . . . The people went away to eat and drink at a festive meal, to share gifts of food, and to celebrate with great joy because they had heard God's words and understood them. NEHEMIAH 8:10, 12

☀ **A prayer about GRACE**
When I wonder what grace means

GRACIOUS GOD,

When I think about grace, I think about doing a big favor for someone without expecting anything in return. You have done me the biggest favor of all—forgiving me for my sins and restoring me to fellowship with you. Thank you! I'm so grateful that I do not have to earn your grace, yet sometimes I still try to prove to you that I'm worthy. Teach me to accept your gift with humility, Lord. May I never forget how much I need you. I can't take credit for your grace any more than a baby can brag about being born. I did nothing to impress you or cause you to love me, but you chose to love me unconditionally. Your grace is a gift, not the product of my own effort. That gives me great comfort and hope, because it also means that I can never lose your grace because of the things I do. I thank you that I am secure in your amazing grace.

God saved you by his grace when you believed. And you can't take credit for this; it is a gift from God. Salvation is not a reward for the good things we have done, so none of us can boast about it. EPHESIANS 2:8-9

☀ A prayer about ENDURANCE
When I need encouragement to run well

LORD JESUS,

The apostle Paul compared life to a race, and that's how it feels sometimes. It's easy to get discouraged and tired, but I need to remember the sense of satisfaction that comes from running well. Help me to endure all the challenges I encounter along the way, and to finish strong. I know that you will reward all those who have faith in you and who endure the challenges of this life—persecution, ridicule, temptation, loss. Someday we will spend eternity with you! I can't think of a better prize. But I can't expect to run this race without training. Teach me to build up endurance so I can live a life of faith in you and stay strong to the end. Then I won't collapse during the race but will be able to push on toward the goal of becoming more and more like you, Jesus. Strengthen me so that someday I will cross the finish line and receive all the eternal rewards you have promised.

Don't you realize that in a race everyone runs, but only one person gets the prize? So run to win! All athletes are disciplined in their training. They do it to win a prize that will fade away, but we do it for an eternal prize. So I run with purpose in every step. 1 CORINTHIANS 9:24-26

☼ A prayer about PAIN
When I wonder if good can come out of pain

LORD,

When I am hurting, I have a choice: I can move away from you or move toward you. I can respond to pain by isolating myself, turning inward, and refusing help, or I can bring my hurt to you and trust you to heal me. One choice only brings me more pain; the other choice brings me healing. Teach me, Lord, that pain is an opportunity to draw near to you. It gives me a chance to see your power as you respond to my cry for help. I know that pain can be redemptive if it leads me back to you, the great healer. Help me to realize that the pain I'm experiencing equips me to comfort others in their pain because I will understand what they are going through. May my hurt not be wasted, but may it teach me how to reach out to those around me. I pray that this painful situation will ultimately strengthen my faith, my character, and my compassion for others.

All praise to God, the Father of our Lord Jesus Christ. God is our merciful Father and the source of all comfort. He comforts us in all our troubles so that we can comfort others. When they are troubled, we will be able to give them the same comfort God has given us. 2 CORINTHIANS 1:3-4

☀ **A prayer about POTENTIAL**
When I want to reach my potential

FATHER,

Teach me to have an honest view of myself. You have given me gifts and abilities, and I'm grateful. Teach me to be neither too proud nor too self-effacing. If I think too highly of myself, I'll forget that I'm supposed to use these gifts for your glory and not my own. Yet if I think too poorly of myself, I'll never have the confidence to use my gifts at all. Help me, Lord, to fulfill the potential you have given me and to have the right attitude as I do it. May I never forget that you are the source of all my abilities and that I should use them for your Kingdom. It's not about me.

Because of the privilege and authority God has given me, I give each of you this warning: Don't think you are better than you really are. Be honest in your evaluation of yourselves, measuring yourselves by the faith God has given us. Just as our bodies have many parts and each part has a special function, so it is with Christ's body. We are many parts of one body, and we all belong to each other.
ROMANS 12:3-5

☼ A prayer about FORGIVENESS
When I have been hurt

LORD,

I've been betrayed by a friend. I want to hold a grudge, but you tell me to forgive as you have forgiven me. No offense against me can ever compare with my own offenses against you. You have wiped clean my debt. How can I withhold forgiveness from someone else? Please give me a merciful heart that is eager to forgive.

Be kind to each other, tenderhearted, forgiving one another, just as God through Christ has forgiven you.
EPHESIANS 4:32

DAY 294 *Prayerful Moment*

☼ A prayer about GUARDING MY HEART
When I need to guard my heart

HEAVENLY FATHER,

I know that my heart is where my actions begin. If I harbor wrong thoughts and attitudes, they will eventually come out in my actions. And the longer I let these wrong thoughts go unchecked, the more my heart will convince me they're okay. Keep me from trusting my emotions to tell me what's right. Instead, help me to trust your Word. I know it comes from your heart, which is good and perfect and will always guide me down the right path.

Guard your heart above all else, for it determines the course of your life. PROVERBS 4:23

⚙ A prayer about ETERNITY
When I need perspective on my problems

ETERNAL GOD,

When I am filled with anxiety because of my circumstances, it's because I forget this world isn't all there is. There's more to my life than what I see today or what will happen in the next twenty years. My future expands much further than that! Give me the eternal perspective that comes from believing that you died on the cross to give me the free gift of eternal life. Thanks to your grace, I know that my eternal future is secure. That gives me peace no matter what is happening right now! May this wonderful truth also change the way I react to the troubles and trials life throws my way. My sinful nature no longer controls me. I praise you that I am free to live the way you want me to live. May the knowledge of the eternity to come with you motivate me to make the most of my time now.

Calling the crowd to join his disciples, [Jesus] said, "If any of you wants to be my follower, you must turn from your selfish ways, take up your cross, and follow me. If you try to hang on to your life, you will lose it. But if you give up your life for my sake and for the sake of the Good News, you will save it." MARK 8:34-35

☼ A prayer about GOD'S WORK
When I wonder how God works in my life

LORD GOD,

Your Word makes clear that some things about you are unchanging. Your love is constant, and so are your promises, your law, and your character. I'm thankful for those rock-solid things I can know without question. Yet I realize that there's so much about you I cannot know. Your character is constant, but your ways are sometimes mysterious. You work both in the world and in my life in a variety of ways, and I can't expect it to always be the same. Teach me to trust your heart even when I can't understand how you're working. Help me to be alert and ready to discover the way you will work through me next. I may not always understand in the moment, but as I look back on past times of my life, I see your fingerprints. I'm thankful that your hand is on me both now and forever.

Oh, how great are God's riches and wisdom and knowledge! How impossible it is for us to understand his decisions and his ways! ROMANS 11:33

☼ **A prayer about MISTAKES**
When I want to learn from my mistakes

FATHER,

I know that everyone makes mistakes, but that doesn't make me feel much better after I've just made a big one. Help me to learn from my mistakes so that I don't repeat them. Often I can avoid repeating a mistake by changing my approach—working harder, planning better, being more careful. But if my mistake is really a sin, I need your help. Teach me to listen to the still, small voice of my conscience. When I feel regret over sin, it's a sign that I want to do something differently—and that's a desire that comes from you. I know that mistakes can have costly consequences, especially if I make the same ones over and over. Please give me spiritual maturity and wisdom from your Word so that I will know better ways to respond to the same situations. I want to grow in my knowledge of you.

We have not stopped praying for you since we first heard about you. We ask God to give you complete knowledge of his will and to give you spiritual wisdom and understanding. Then the way you live will always honor and please the Lord, and your lives will produce every kind of good fruit. All the while, you will grow as you learn to know God better and better. COLOSSIANS 1:9-10

☼ A prayer about MY PAST
When I wonder how to move on from my past

LORD GOD,

When I think about my life so far as a collection of snap-shots, I see many happy moments and celebrations. But I also see failures, tragedies, embarrassing moments, and choices that cause me great shame. I would love to lock away parts of my past or tear those photos out of the collection. But my past is past. I can't change it, so I need to figure out how to move beyond it. Help me to look to the apostle Paul for motivation. After all, he had some pretty awful snapshots in his past—persecuting and killing Christians. He could have spent the rest of his life regretting what he'd done, but instead he understood that you had redeemed his past through your healing and forgiveness. Thank you that you can redeem mine, too. When I am stuck thinking about an incident in my past, teach me to deal with any unconfessed sin in my life and then turn it over to you. Remind me that it is over and done. I place it in your hands, knowing that you can make even the worst things in my past work for your glory in the present and future.

[The Lord says,] "Though your sins are like scarlet, I will make them as white as snow. Though they are red like crimson, I will make them as white as wool." ISAIAH 1:18

☼ A prayer about WAITING
When things aren't moving as quickly as I'd like

LORD,

It's difficult to wait for many things—for my food to come at a restaurant, for a response to an application, for the results of a theater audition, for another person to be ready to reconcile with me, or for you to work in my life in a certain way. Please give me patience as I am waiting. Teach me to trust that you have my best interests at heart, and that in this case, delay might be better for me. I know that the path you lead me on may be longer and slower than the one I wish for, but it may be for my own protection and provision that you don't give me immediate victory. Impress on my heart that time spent waiting is never wasted by you. You are using this period of waiting in my life to prepare me for what's ahead. As I wait, may I serve you where I am and draw near to you.

I am confident I will see the LORD's goodness while I am
here in the land of the living. Wait patiently for the LORD.
Be brave and courageous. Yes, wait patiently for the LORD.
PSALM 27:13-14

DAY 300 *Prayerful Moment*

☀ A prayer about FORGIVENESS
When I am amazed by God's forgiveness

LORD,

When I read the promises in your Word about forgiveness, I am amazed. You tell me that you will blot out my sins completely and never think of them again! Human forgiveness can never come close to that. Even when I say I forgive someone, I find myself remembering the offense. But you promise never to mull over my wrongs. When you forgive me, you wash me totally, completely clean. Thank you, God!

[The Lord says,] "I—yes, I alone—will blot out your sins for my own sake and will never think of them again."
ISAIAH 43:25

DAY 301 *Prayerful Moment*

☀ A prayer about RELEVANCE
When others question if the Bible is relevant today

FATHER,

A lot of people around me think the Bible is totally irrelevant. They wonder how I can take it seriously or think it has anything to say to me. Yet I believe your Word is true, living, and active. I believe it speaks to me today. When I read it I find wisdom, peace, comfort, and direction. How can that not be relevant? May my heart always be open to your Word. I know it has the power to transform my life.

The grass withers and the flowers fade, but the word of our God stands forever. ISAIAH 40:8

☼ A prayer about PERSECUTION
*When I want to pray for believers experiencing
persecution*

LORD GOD,

So many Christians around the world are dealing with persecution on a level I can't even imagine. Some people are disowned by their families for putting their faith in Christ. Others are subject to arrest or punishment just for being part of a church. O Lord, make your presence known to these believers. Comfort them, encourage them, and strengthen them as they face these trials. Ease their suffering. I pray that their faith in you will grow, not weaken, as a result of the persecution they endure. May their faith be a shining example of your power and love both to their persecutors and to the church around the world. Show me what I can do to encourage better treatment of Christians in other countries. Help me to remember these believers regularly in prayer. May they know they are not forgotten.

The more we suffer for Christ, the more God will shower us with his comfort through Christ. 2 CORINTHIANS 1:5

DAY 303

☀ A prayer about REGRETS
When I am weighed down by guilt and regret

LORD,

My guilt and regret weigh heavily on me today. I feel guilt over my sin and regret over the consequences of my past decisions. I wish I could take back some of the things I have done, but I know that all my remorse cannot change the past. Please help me deal with my regrets so that I can move forward without carrying such a heavy load of guilt. Thank you for forgiving all my sins when I ask. You promise to forget the past and give me a fresh start. You no longer hold my sins against me, so teach me, Lord, not to hold them against myself. Free me from this load of self-condemnation. May my regrets never enslave me so fully that they consume my thoughts and disable me from serving you. Instead, let me realize that your forgiveness changes everything. May that motivate me to positive action in the future. Turn my regrets into resolve.

Oh, what joy for those whose disobedience is forgiven, whose sin is put out of sight! Yes, what joy for those whose record the LORD has cleared of guilt, whose lives are lived in complete honesty! PSALM 32:1-2

☼ A prayer about EMPTINESS
When I'm searching for meaning

O GOD,

I feel so empty. I try to satisfy myself with possessions, busyness, and even people, but in those moments when I'm alone and still, the emptiness creeps back in. It's like eating junk food—it makes me full for a while, but very soon I'm hungry again. I wonder what I'm really accomplishing with my life, what the future holds, and why I don't feel a stronger sense of purpose. Help me not to fight against this feeling of emptiness. It's there to make me realize my need for you. You are the only one who can fulfill me, giving me your love and a passion for your Kingdom. My heart is like an empty room, waiting to be occupied. Fill my heart with your Holy Spirit, Lord! I invite you in.

May you experience the love of Christ, though it is too great to understand fully. Then you will be made complete with all the fullness of life and power that comes from God.
EPHESIANS 3:19

☼ A prayer about RESPECT
When I want others to respect me

LORD,

I want to be a person who receives respect. Is it wrong to want to be in a position of authority and have others look up to me? Test my motives, Lord, and teach me the right keys to earning respect. When I read your Word, it's clear that respect comes from serving rather than being served, from taking responsibility instead of trying to save face, from speaking up when things are wrong rather than going along with the crowd. When I build others up instead of trying to make myself look good, I'm worthy of respect. The world around me tells me that my appearance, popularity, and accomplishments are the keys to respect. But I need your help to remember that this kind of admiration is transient; it will last only until someone more attractive, more popular, or more accomplished comes along. Please help me to pursue the characteristics that are genuinely worthy of lasting respect: kindness, integrity, and a deep love for others.

There will be glory and honor and peace from God for all who do good. ROMANS 2:10

☼ A prayer about FLEXIBILITY
When I need to be more flexible

HEAVENLY FATHER,

I want to be used by you. But that means that I need to be available, and I need to be willing to respond when you speak to me. Teach me to be more flexible. It's easy for me to get caught up in whatever I think I need to do right now and to ignore everything else. But I know that sometimes it's the unexpected opportunities to serve you or encourage someone else that can be the most fruitful. Show me that being flexible will allow me to avoid anything that might take my focus off you. Then I'll be able to devote myself to you with all my heart and be ready when you call. Bless me and use me, Lord, not only because of my ability but because of my availability.

Be dressed for service and keep your lamps burning, as though you were waiting for your master to return from the wedding feast. Then you will be ready to open the door and let him in the moment he arrives and knocks. The servants who are ready and waiting for his return will be rewarded.
LUKE 12:35-37

☼ A prayer about BETRAYAL
When I have been hurt by a friend

LORD,

I need your help to deal with the betrayal I'm feeling. A friend has hurt me, and I feel like taking revenge. Calm me, Lord. Help me to realize that the best thing I can do is to stop the cycle of retaliation by offering love instead of vengeance. I don't need to justify myself or show that I'm right. I trust you to judge my case.

Dear friends, never take revenge. Leave that to the righteous anger of God. . . . Don't let evil conquer you, but conquer evil by doing good. ROMANS 12:19, 21

DAY 308 *Prayerful Moment*

☼ A prayer about RELATIONSHIPS
When I'm amazed by God's love

LORD,

No relationship I'll ever have on earth can completely reflect the kind of relationship you want to have with me. Sometimes your Word uses images of the love between a husband and wife or a parent and child, but I know those illustrations can only give me a glimpse of what your love is really like. I'm amazed at the unconditional love you shower on me. You want to make me the best I can be. You want to spend eternity with me. Thank you, Lord!

See how very much our Father loves us, for he calls us his children. 1 JOHN 3:1

☀ **A prayer about EVIL**
When I wonder why God allows evil in the world

HEAVENLY FATHER,

This world is so broken. When I look around me, I see hurt and difficulty and sickness everywhere. Why does there have to be evil in the world? How I wish you would just wipe it clean and save me from all the trouble I face on earth. Yet I know that the world is like this because you gave humans the freedom to choose. I can choose you or I can choose my own way, and when I choose my own way, it always leads to sin. Yet you allow me that choice because you love me and want a relationship with me. If I had to do things your way, I would be coerced—and that's not love. Because you love people so much, it must break your heart to look at the world and see all the ways we hurt each other. But someday you will destroy the power of evil forever. And until then, I can continue to make choices each day. May I choose your way today!

The LORD God placed the man in the Garden of Eden to tend and watch over it. But the LORD God warned him, "You may freely eat the fruit of every tree in the garden— except the tree of the knowledge of good and evil. If you eat its fruit, you are sure to die." GENESIS 2:15-17

☼ A prayer about QUITTING
When I feel like giving up

LORD GOD,

I'm tired and frustrated, and I need the wisdom to know when to quit. Teach me not to give up on something only because I'm discouraged. After all, just because something is worthwhile doesn't mean it will be easy. But sometimes the things I put my efforts into are just not worthwhile. Show me that it's time to quit when I'm doing something wrong, when my actions are futile, or when I'm hurting myself or others. Even if my actions aren't wrong, it might be time to quit if what I'm doing isn't productive, if it's taking up too much of my time and energy, or if it causes other believers to stumble in some way. Please give me discernment as I evaluate my actions. When I know I'm working on something good and worthwhile that you've set before me, give me the perseverance to keep going. May I be bold and faithful as I work for you.

We are pressed on every side by troubles, but we are not crushed. We are perplexed, but not driven to despair. . . . We know that God, who raised the Lord Jesus, will also raise us with Jesus and present us to himself together with you. . . . That is why we never give up. 2 CORINTHIANS 4:8, 14, 16

☼ **A prayer about THE RESURRECTION**
When I wonder about our resurrected bodies

LORD,

Today I'm thinking a lot about the Resurrection. When I look at the older people around me, I see the way their bodies are starting to break down. Physical tasks that used to be simple are becoming more and more difficult. And I know even younger people who are struggling with serious illness, chronic pain, or depression. When I get discouraged by this physical failure, help me to remember that these earthly bodies are only temporary. Thank you that someday all believers will have resurrected bodies. They will never decay from the effects of sin. I'll never be sick or feel pain again, and my mind won't think sinful thoughts. I'll never again compare myself with other people or wish that I had been created differently. What freedom that will be! I will be fully and finally perfect in your sight. I praise you, Lord, for giving me this amazing gift for eternity. May the truth of the resurrection encourage me and motivate me today.

Our earthly bodies are planted in the ground when we die, but they will be raised to live forever. Our bodies are buried in brokenness, but they will be raised in glory. They are buried in weakness, but they will be raised in strength.

I CORINTHIANS 15:42-43

☼ A prayer about LISTENING
When I need to listen to others

HEAVENLY FATHER,

Now that I'm becoming more independent, I sometimes think that I no longer need to listen to my parents or anyone else. I want to be considered an adult and do things my own way. But your Word tells me to listen to those who are wise because I can learn from them. Please give me a spirit of humility to guard me from thinking that I know everything. Help me to be willing to listen to those who have more experience than I do. Your truth is found in your Word, which is available to all, but I know others have insight into how it should be applied. Teach me to honor others by listening to them with attention and respect. May my ears be open to the wisdom I will gain from others.

My child, listen when your father corrects you. Don't neglect your mother's instruction. What you learn from them will crown you with grace and be a chain of honor around your neck. PROVERBS 1:8-9

☼ A prayer about EXPECTATIONS
When God challenges my expectations

LORD GOD,

Your ways are beyond my ways, and your thoughts are beyond my thoughts. So why am I surprised when you do the opposite of what I expect? Your Word is full of examples. You chose David, the youngest son in his family and a lowly shepherd, to be the king of Israel. You took Saul, the most vicious opponent of the early church, and transformed him into Paul, the greatest missionary of all time. You cared for women in a time when they had no rights. You even took the cross, an object of torture and ultimate defeat, and made it the sign of victory over sin and death for all eternity! I praise you for your creativity, which knows no bounds. Forgive me for limiting you to my own understanding and expectations. Thank you for surprising me in ways that inspire my awe, love, gratitude, and joy.

He gave up his divine privileges; he took the humble position of a slave and was born as a human being. When he appeared in human form, he humbled himself in obedience to God and died a criminal's death on a cross. Therefore, God elevated him to the place of highest honor and gave him the name above all other names. PHILIPPIANS 2:7-9

☼ **A prayer about MUSIC**
  When I want to praise God through music

GOD,

Thank you for the beauty of music. It touches my heart in a way that simple words cannot, and it gives me a glimpse into your awesome, creative beauty. Teach me to worship meaningfully, Lord, through both music and lyrics. May I give you praise and express my faith as I sing.

Those who have been ransomed by the LORD will return. They will enter Jerusalem singing, crowned with everlasting joy. Sorrow and mourning will disappear, and they will be filled with joy and gladness. ISAIAH 51:11

☼ **A prayer about FRIENDSHIP**
  When I want to cultivate friendships

LORD,

Without good friends, life can feel empty. I'm grateful for the friends I have who care for me, who look out for me when things are hard, who encourage me in my faith, and who give me joy. I want to grow these friendships and add even more. Help me to be a good and loyal friend to others, loving them unconditionally and seeking what's best for them. Thank you for the gift of friendship—and for being the best friend of all.

A friend is always loyal, and a brother is born to help in time of need. PROVERBS 17:17

☼ **A prayer about TEMPTATION**
When I am tempted

LORD,

How can I handle the pressure I feel when I am tempted to sin? Teach me first to acknowledge that what I want to do is sinful—not just a little mistake or a choice I can justify. Admitting that is the first step. Then help me to stand firm in my commitment to you. I want to please you with the way I live; I don't want to fall into sin. Give me the willpower to avoid areas of temptation or even run away from compromising situations if I need to. I know that Satan always strikes where I am weakest. Please help me recognize my areas of vulnerability so I won't be surprised when temptation knocks at my door. Teach me to watch for it and pray for the strength to resist it. Then when it comes, I'll be prepared to say no.

The temptations in your life are no different from what others experience. And God is faithful. He will not allow the temptation to be more than you can stand. When you are tempted, he will show you a way out so that you can endure.
I CORINTHIANS 10:13

☀ A prayer about EXAMPLE
When I want to be a role model for others

LORD JESUS,

I want to set a good example for others. I want my friends and acquaintances to have a good opinion of my character. What kind of qualities should be my goal? First, please teach me to have a servant's heart—to seek ways to help others rather than acting as if I'm more important than anyone else. Help me to take responsibility for my actions, never blaming others when things don't go my way. Give me the courage to speak up when something is unjust or when a wrong is being committed, and keep me humble so I am never motivated by pride. The world teaches me to look and act cool, to bend the rules, to disrespect authority. But I know your Word teaches the opposite, and your standards are what will last. I want to receive honor and respect, so I commit to living a life of kindness, integrity, and love for you. As I strive to do this, please shape my character into your image.

Jesus called them together and said, "You know that the rulers in this world lord it over their people, and officials flaunt their authority over those under them. But among you it will be different. Whoever wants to be a leader among you must be your servant, and whoever wants to be first among you must become your slave. For even the Son of Man came not to be served but to serve others and to give his life as a ransom for many." MATTHEW 20:25-28

⚙ **A prayer about AUTHENTICITY**
   When I want my faith to be real

GOD,

I don't want to go through the motions, pretending my faith is vibrant when it's really weak. I want my faith to be living, real, and strong enough to change my life. Teach me that being authentic means doing the right thing because I really want to, not pretending to do it so I can get what I want. Please work in my heart so that your truth will go deeper and deeper. May I be genuinely grieved by my sins, may I long for a vibrant relationship with you, and may I turn from the corruption in my life and stop doing what is wrong. Give me the courage to be honest with you and others about both my failures and my successes. Then my faith will be authentic, affecting every aspect of my life. I pray that others will see the genuineness of my faith and seek after you.

Let your roots grow down into him, and let your lives be built on him. Then your faith will grow strong in the truth you were taught, and you will overflow with thankfulness.
COLOSSIANS 2:7

☼ A prayer about SIGNIFICANCE
When I feel unimportant

LORD,

I long for significance. I want my life to count, to make a difference, to be worth something. Yet everywhere I look, I see others who are more successful, more gifted, more outgoing, more attractive . . . the list goes on. How can I make a difference in this world? I'm comforted when I read your Word and see that the heroes of the faith were just ordinary people. Moses was afraid to speak to Pharaoh, Gideon thought he was too unimportant to lead an army, and Peter made blunder after blunder—but you used them anyway. Teach me that my significance comes not from what I can accomplish with my abilities but from what *you* can accomplish through my abilities. You gave me significance when you created me. You love me, and I am valuable in your sight. Help me to look to you to find my purpose in life. I know you can use me for great things if I am available to you.

Moses pleaded with the LORD, "O Lord, I'm not very good with words. I never have been, and I'm not now, even though you have spoken to me. I get tongue-tied, and my words get tangled." Then the LORD asked Moses, "Who makes a person's mouth? Who decides whether people speak or do not speak, hear or do not hear, see or do not see? Is it not I, the LORD? Now go! I will be with you as you speak, and I will instruct you in what to say." EXODUS 4:10-12

☼ A prayer about FEAR
When I am afraid

POWERFUL GOD,

I am afraid, and my problems seem so big. I don't see a way around them, but I hold to the truth that you are bigger than any problem. I remember the story from your Word about the Israelite spies who scouted the Promised Land. You had promised the people that they would conquer the land, yet when the spies reported how strong its inhabitants were, the Israelites gave in to fear. The threat seemed so much more immediate than your promise. I don't want to respond to my problems that way, Lord. Help me to remember that fear keeps me from seeing things clearly. When I face a "giant"—whether it's temptation, guilt, anxiety, sin, anger, depression, or something else—help me always to remember that it is not a giant to you. No matter what I feel, you are more powerful than any obstacle in my life, and you have promised to deliver me.

"We entered the land you sent us to explore, and it is indeed a bountiful country—a land flowing with milk and honey. Here is the kind of fruit it produces. But the people living there are powerful, and their towns are large and fortified. We even saw giants there."... Caleb tried to quiet the people as they stood before Moses. "Let's go at once to take the land," he said. "We can certainly conquer it!" But the other men who had explored the land with him disagreed. "We can't go up against them! They are stronger than we are!" NUMBERS 13:27-28, 30-31

✿ **A prayer about MIRACLES**
   When I wonder if God still does miracles

ALMIGHTY GOD,

May I never be blind to the mighty works you are doing right before my eyes. They may not be as dramatic as the miracles I read about in your Word, but they are still happening all around me. The healing of an illness, the restoration of a hopeless relationship, the rebirth of the earth in the spring, and the transformation of my heart are just a few of the incredible ways you act in your creation. Give me eyes to see your wonderful works.

Come and see what our God has done, what awesome miracles he performs for people! PSALM 66:5

DAY 322 *Prayerful Moment*

✿ **A prayer about INTEGRITY**
   When I want to live an upright life

LORD GOD,

I want to be known as a person of integrity. I don't want to cut corners or act hypocritically. Instead, I want my actions and my character to be consistent with my beliefs. Help me to build integrity each day through the choices I make. May my words and actions be honest and dependable, so that others will know they can count on me to do what I say I will.

To the faithful you show yourself faithful; to those with integrity you show integrity. 2 SAMUEL 22:26

⚙ A prayer about TRUST
When I am thankful that God is trustworthy

LORD,

Few things in this world are wholly trustworthy. Even the people I love most can let me down sometimes, but you never will. Your word is reliable; your promises will come true; your love will never fail. Thank you! I'm so grateful that I can trust in what you say—that Jesus died to save me from my sins and rose again from the dead, that you have a plan for my life, you love me eternally, that you have a place prepared for me in heaven. Encourage me with this knowledge, I pray. May it prepare me to step out in faith and let you lead me wherever you want me to go. You are faithful, and I know that I can trust you.

Your unfailing love, O LORD, is as vast as the heavens; your faithfulness reaches beyond the clouds. Your righteousness is like the mighty mountains, your justice like the ocean depths. You care for people and animals alike, O LORD. How precious is your unfailing love, O God! All humanity finds shelter in the shadow of your wings. PSALM 36:5-7

☼ A prayer about COMPARISONS
When I wonder how I measure up

LORD JESUS,

I waste a lot of time and energy comparing myself to other people. Am I smarter, better-looking, or more well-liked than the other people in the room? Am I at least above average? It's exhausting to constantly be wondering if I measure up. Teach me, too, that it can lead to sinful thoughts. If I think I'm better than someone else, it leads to pride and selfishness. If I don't think I'm as good as someone else, it leads to jealousy and discouragement. Either way, my focus is on myself instead of on you. Please help me to stop comparing myself to other people and start comparing myself to your standards. Then I'll know both that I fall short and that your grace is enough to make me holy in your eyes. Remind me that you value every person on earth, no matter how we look or how much we accomplish. May your grace be enough for me.

Pay careful attention to your own work, for then you will get the satisfaction of a job well done, and you won't need to compare yourself to anyone else. For we are each responsible for our own conduct. GALATIANS 6:4-5

☀ **A prayer about SPIRITUAL DISCIPLINE**
*When I want spiritual disciplines to become part
of my life*

LORD,

I see athletes training over and over again so that funda-
mental skills will become second nature to them. Please
teach me to practice spiritual disciplines in the same
way. May following you become an automatic reflex that
will guard my heart when I face temptation. May prayer
become such an ingrained habit that I will automatically
turn to you in any crisis. May meditating on your Word
become so much a part of me that Scripture passages will
come to mind when I most need direction. I pray for the
willpower to pursue these disciplines with an undivided
heart, out of my love for you.

*I have hidden your word in my heart, that I might not sin
against you. I praise you, O LORD; teach me your decrees.
I have recited aloud all the regulations you have given us. I
have rejoiced in your laws as much as in riches. I will study
your commandments and reflect on your ways. I will delight
in your decrees and not forget your word.* PSALM 119:11-16

☀ **A prayer about GENTLENESS**
When I need God's help to be gentle

FATHER,

I don't think about gentleness too often. It's not highly prized in my culture; people are more interested in verbal jabs and one-upmanship than genuine kindness. And when I consider my interactions with other people, I'm not sure I see much gentleness in my life either. Being gentle takes time and effort. It's much easier for me to be abrupt or harsh instead of kind and careful. Yet your Word makes clear that you have called me to gentleness. Please create in me a gentle spirit that will delight to treat others with honor and care. May I remember how gentle you have been to me, kindly guiding me down the right path. Show me how to express that gentle love to those around me. Transform my words, my tone, and my body language as I try to exhibit gentleness in every interaction.

Since God chose you to be the holy people he loves, you must clothe yourselves with tenderhearted mercy, kindness, humility, gentleness, and patience. Make allowance for each other's faults, and forgive anyone who offends you. Remember, the Lord forgave you, so you must forgive others. Above all, clothe yourselves with love, which binds us all together in perfect harmony. COLOSSIANS 3:12-14

☼ A prayer about CONFESSION
When I need to confess my sin to God

LORD,

I know I should never try to hide sin from you. When I'm struggling with sin, please give me the courage to talk to you and possibly to an accountability partner as well. When I keep myself in isolation, sin begins to fester, and it will only get worse—sapping my energy, distracting me, depriving me of creativity and passion. Teach me that confession is one of the first steps toward renewal. May I always be humble and honest with you, sincerely sorry for my sins and responsive when you uncover more wrongdoing in my life. Then my relationship with you will be renewed. You will remove my guilt, restore my joy, turn me in the right direction, and heal my broken soul. O Lord, may I never miss out on the restoration that comes from genuine confession.

When I refused to confess my sin, my body wasted away, and I groaned all day long. Day and night your hand of discipline was heavy on me. My strength evaporated like water in the summer heat. Finally, I confessed all my sins to you and stopped trying to hide my guilt. I said to myself, "I will confess my rebellion to the LORD." And you forgave me! All my guilt is gone. PSALM 32:3-5

✷ **A prayer about GOD'S POWER**
When I am weak

ALMIGHTY GOD,

I am weak, but you are strong. And your Word tells me that your power is made perfect in weakness! When I am struggling, I know that it is only through your strength that I can accomplish anything. Thank you for working in me and through me with your mighty power.

Each time he said, "My grace is all you need. My power works best in weakness." So now I am glad to boast about my weaknesses, so that the power of Christ can work through me.
2 CORINTHIANS 12:9

DAY 329 *Prayerful Moment*

✷ **A prayer about PURPOSE**
When I am looking for meaning

LORD,

I'm grateful that you have a purpose for my life. You want me to become more like you! And as I do, you want the love of Jesus to shine through me and have an impact on others. Thank you for giving my life meaning and significance. May I pursue these goals with all my heart, for your glory through eternity.

My life is worth nothing to me unless I use it for finishing the work assigned me by the Lord Jesus—the work of telling others the Good News about the wonderful grace of God.
ACTS 20:24

☼ A prayer about DISTRACTIONS
When I am frustrated by things that distract me from my goal

LORD JESUS,

When I'm motivated to finish a project or meet a goal, I get frustrated by distractions. Yet your Word tells me that when you were on earth, you treated interruptions as opportunities to save the lost or help people in need. When the disciples scolded parents for daring to bring their little children to you, you rebuked them and then took the time to bless each child. Help me to follow your example, Lord Jesus. Forgive me for reacting in frustration to people who need my help. Instead, teach me to take a deep breath, pause from my task, and take the time to express your love. May I never miss the opportunities you put in my path.

One day some parents brought their children to Jesus so he could lay his hands on them and pray for them. But the disciples scolded the parents for bothering him. But Jesus said, "Let the children come to me. Don't stop them! For the Kingdom of Heaven belongs to those who are like these children." And he placed his hands on their heads and blessed them before he left. MATTHEW 19:13-15

☼ A prayer about FAMILY
When I am thankful for my family

HEAVENLY FATHER,

In this time of my life I'm becoming more independent, so I'm relying less on my family to meet my physical needs. Yet in a way, now that I have a little more distance, I'm even more thankful for them. My family isn't perfect. But even so, I'm grateful for the role they have played in my life so far. Thank you for the gift of family—those who live close by and those who are far away. Thanks for people who have known me all my life and care about me deeply. And Lord, I'm so grateful for you, too. When I've had struggles with my family or they have failed me in some way, you have been there to fill the gaps. Your love is rock-solid and will never leave me. I am so glad to be your child.

You received God's Spirit when he adopted you as his own children. Now we call him, "Abba, Father." For his Spirit joins with our spirit to affirm that we are God's children. And since we are his children, we are his heirs.
ROMANS 8:15-17

☼ **A prayer about CONFLICT**
When I'm not sure how to handle strife

LORD JESUS,

It's hard to handle conflict the right way. Too often my tendency is either to pretend the problem isn't there or to blow up at the other person involved. I need you to show me a better way. Teach me that my goal is to resolve conflict, not to ignore or exacerbate it. Help me to understand that resolving conflict takes initiative, humility, and persistence. To do it, I need to want peace more than I want to win. That will require a major heart change, Lord. Please remove my pride and turn my heart toward peace. When someone disagrees with me, show me how to have a gracious, gentle, and patient attitude instead of becoming angry or defensive. Help me to remember your example and reach out to my opponent in love. Then the conflict will become secondary to the opportunity to express your love to those around me.

A servant of the Lord must not quarrel but must be kind to everyone, be able to teach, and be patient with difficult people. Gently instruct those who oppose the truth. Perhaps God will change those people's hearts, and they will learn the truth. 2 TIMOTHY 2:24-25

DAY 333

☼ A prayer about ENCOURAGEMENT
When I want to encourage others

LORD,

When I look back on my life, I can think of specific words from others that have encouraged me. Maybe one person told me he saw potential in me, and another showed that she cared when I was going through a tough time. Someone else encouraged me to be diligent in studying the Bible. Words are so powerful, and I want to use mine to encourage others. Please teach me to speak words that are positive, wholesome, and helpful. Show me how to share truth from your Word that will remind others of how much you love them. Help me to be thoughtful enough to compliment others for a job well done or notice when they are struggling. May my words build others up and encourage them in their walk with you.

Don't use foul or abusive language. Let everything you say be good and helpful, so that your words will be an encouragement to those who hear them. EPHESIANS 4:29

⚙ **A prayer about DEPENDENCE**
When I need to depend more fully on God

LORD,

I want to live with a constant sense of your presence. Sometimes it's only when I'm getting ready for bed at night that I realize I haven't thought about you all day. Then I'm ashamed. Teach me to be aware of my total dependence on you. Help me to live in a moment-by-moment conversation with you, even as I go about my daily tasks. Especially in the morning, may I set aside time to think about how much I need your help for the day ahead. In the evening, let me take time to think about how you have helped me throughout the day. As I become more aware of your presence, please grow in me the self-discipline to focus on you until you are a part of my every moment. I need you.

Blessed are those who trust in the LORD and have made the LORD their hope and confidence. They are like trees planted along a riverbank, with roots that reach deep into the water. Such trees are not bothered by the heat or worried by long months of drought. Their leaves stay green, and they never stop producing fruit. JEREMIAH 17:7-8

☼ A prayer about TRUTH
When I need to be fully truthful

LORD GOD,

It's easy to fudge the truth sometimes when I'm feeling embarrassed or threatened. Often it comes down to my wanting others' approval. Yet I know that relationships fall apart without trust. I never want my friends and acquaintances to doubt my word, Lord. I want to be trustworthy. Guard my lips and awaken my conscience so that I will be aware of when I'm bending the truth. May each word that comes out of my mouth meet your standard for truth.

Truthful words stand the test of time, but lies are soon exposed.
PROVERBS 12:19

DAY 336 *Prayerful Moment*

☼ A prayer about CONFIDENCE
When I want to gain self-assurance

LORD,

I want to be confident, certain that I'm valuable in your sight and headed in the right direction. Teach me that having confidence in myself only comes from having confidence in you. May I never doubt your Word or your love for me. Then I can be confident and fearless.

Those who are righteous will be long remembered. They do not fear bad news; they confidently trust the LORD to care for them. They are confident and fearless and can face their foes triumphantly. PSALM 112:6-8

☼ A prayer about CONSEQUENCES
When I'm experiencing consequences of my actions

LORD GOD,

How I wish you would swoop in and save me every time I mess up. But I know if you did that, I would never learn. I would become spoiled, not caring if I hurt others because I would never feel any remorse for what I did. That's not what you want for me, and if I'm honest, that's not what I want for myself either. Thank you that even though you don't take away the consequences of my bad choices, you do heal the hurt—both in my life and in the life of anyone I've wronged. You do this through the power of forgiveness. Give me the humility to ask forgiveness of anyone I've hurt. When I do, you will begin a miraculous process of healing in our relationship. Thank you! It would be a terrible world if our hurts never went away. You are so gracious to bring reconciliation and new life—both to my human relationships and to my relationship with you. Teach me that although admitting my mistakes may be humbling and painful in the short term, in the long term it will bring beauty and new life.

If we confess our sins to him, he is faithful and just to forgive us our sins and to cleanse us from all wickedness.
I JOHN 1:9

☼ A prayer about IMPACT
When I want to have a positive influence on others

FATHER,

I'm surrounded by so many people in my neighborhood, at work, and in my other activities, and many of them need you. I want to have a positive impact on them. Help me to remember that the best way to do that is to reflect your character. When I see people who are full of your love, wisdom, and truthfulness, I'm drawn to them. May others see those characteristics in me! I pray that my friends and neighbors would be drawn to me not necessarily because I'm fun or smart—but because they can see that you are with me. Lord, I will count it an honor and privilege if you use my life to bless others and draw them to you.

You must worship Christ as Lord of your life. And if someone asks about your Christian hope, always be ready to explain it. But do this in a gentle and respectful way. Keep your conscience clear. Then if people speak against you, they will be ashamed when they see what a good life you live because you belong to Christ. 1 PETER 3:15-16

DAY 339

☼ A prayer about UNITY
When I need to work with others

LORD,

Thank you for the variety of people you have made in this world. We are not all alike, and that's a good thing! We have differences of opinion, differences of perspective, and differences in personality. I can celebrate that. But when we need to work together in pursuit of a common goal, things sometimes get tricky. Teach me how to work toward unity. I know that doesn't mean we all have to have the same view, just that we need to work as a team to reach a certain objective. As we decide how to do that, I pray for the humility to acknowledge that my opinions may not be the best ones. Help me to listen to others and be open to new ideas. May I not get distracted by trying to get my way in the process, but instead set my eyes on the final goal. Thank you for designing us to share and enjoy unity.

Make every effort to keep yourselves united in the Spirit, binding yourselves together with peace. For there is one body and one Spirit, just as you have been called to one glorious hope for the future. EPHESIANS 4:3-4

☼ A prayer about ADDICTION
When I need help to face my addictions

LORD JESUS,

I'm ready to admit that my addiction is beyond my control. It may be to a substance, like drugs or alcohol, or to a harmful behavior, but it's destructive and I want to be free of it. I can't do it by myself. I need you, Lord! Please take control of my life. Keep me close to you and change my heart and my desires. Teach me to surrender to your Holy Spirit so that you can replace my addictive impulses with desires that will give me new life. I know you can also use other people to help me. Direct me to those who love me enough to tell me the truth and hold me accountable. Give me the courage to trust them so that I can move forward with support and confidence. With your help, I know I can overcome this addiction.

You are not controlled by your sinful nature. You are controlled by the Spirit if you have the Spirit of God living in you.
ROMANS 8:9

❋ A prayer about PREPARATION
When I wonder if I'm ready for what's ahead

HEAVENLY FATHER,

I'm thankful that when you call me to a task, you equip me for it. You promise to give me the resources to complete whatever work you ask me to do. Teach me that you give me counsel and direction through your Word, special abilities and gifts to use, and your Holy Spirit to give me strength and guidance along the way. You will never leave me unprepared. When I feel unready or unsure, help me to remember that you are on my team. You want me to succeed because I am doing your work and because you love me. Thank you, Lord.

Now may the God of peace—who brought up from the dead our Lord Jesus, the great Shepherd of the sheep, and ratified an eternal covenant with his blood—may he equip you with all you need for doing his will. May he produce in you, through the power of Jesus Christ, every good thing that is pleasing to him. HEBREWS 13:20-21

☼ A prayer about DISCOURAGEMENT
When I am at the end of my rope

FATHER GOD,

I call out to you today, knowing that you hear me and you share my burdens. I feel lost and discouraged. Let me feel your presence. Thank you for allowing me to be honest with you. Thank you for never leaving me alone. I can count on you to strengthen me, comfort me, and give me the courage I need to get through this crisis.

Why am I discouraged? Why is my heart so sad? I will put my hope in God! I will praise him again—my Savior and my God! PSALM 42:5-6

☼ A prayer about ADVICE
When I wonder if I'm getting the right counsel

FATHER,

I'm surrounded by people who want to give me advice. But I know their advice is not always the same as wise counsel. Only your wisdom is perfect, because you alone are all-knowing. Teach me, Lord, to seek knowledge and understanding from you, the only one who knows everything that will happen today and tomorrow and every day to come. All wisdom comes from you.

The LORD says, "I will guide you along the best pathway for your life. I will advise you and watch over you."
PSALM 32:8

☼ A prayer about CRITICISM
When I am critical of others

LORD,

When I think I know the right way to do something, it's hard to bite back the words when I see another person doing it differently. Yet I need to remember that most of the time it's not my place to judge someone else. Your Word tells me to look first at myself before I look critically at another. When I am in a leadership position or have the opportunity to offer constructive criticism, teach me to do it in the spirit of love. May I never ridicule or demean someone else, causing him or her to become defensive. Instead, may I approach the situation with humility and understanding. Help me to carefully consider my own motives. Am I criticizing the other person because I want to look important, or do I genuinely want to help him or her improve and grow? Teach me to take inventory of my own sins and shortcomings before I try to guide someone else.

First get rid of the log in your own eye; then you will see well enough to deal with the speck in your friend's eye.
MATTHEW 7:5

⚜ A prayer about ACCOUNTABILITY
When I don't want to be held accountable

FATHER,

Sometimes I don't like the sound of accountability. I don't always want to give an account of myself—where I've been, what I've been doing, or what my motives are. I want to be in charge of my life! But I know that everyone needs accountability. Help me to remember that its purpose isn't to keep me from having fun but to help me enjoy life even more by preventing me from doing something that will hurt myself or someone else. Direct me to the people in my life who can hold me accountable, and teach me that I am always accountable to you. As I fill my mind with your guidance from Scripture, please guard my heart and keep me on the right path.

You must commit yourselves wholeheartedly to these commands that I am giving you today. Repeat them again and again to your children. Talk about them when you are at home and when you are on the road, when you are going to bed and when you are getting up. DEUTERONOMY 6:6-7

☼ A prayer about COMMUNITY
When I need connection with other believers

LORD,

I'm thankful for my friends and even more thankful for the community I find among other believers. Teach me to value this kind of fellowship because it invites you, the living God, into our midst. Thank you for giving me the opportunity to be a part of a group of believers who also know their sins have been forgiven, have experienced the joy of salvation, and have a future together in heaven. I pray that we would provide each other a safe place to share honestly about the things that really matter in life. Help us to encourage one another to stay strong in the midst of temptation and persecution, and to seek wisdom together for the problems we face. Keep us from becoming a closed, inwardly focused group; rather, give us the courage to share the love in our fellowship with others who need it— and need you. Thank you for the gift of community.

If we are living in the light, as God is in the light, then we have fellowship with each other, and the blood of Jesus, his Son, cleanses us from all sin. 1 JOHN 1:7

☀ A prayer about DECISIONS
When I wonder how to make good choices

ALMIGHTY GOD,

I'm faced with so many decisions, and I need some guidelines that will help me make good ones. Teach me first of all to make decisions with humility and out of reverence for you. I know that acknowledging my need for your wisdom is the foundation for any good choice. Help me also to avoid making decisions solely out of a desire for personal gain. Out of love, I need to consider how my choices impact those around me. I want to develop wisdom, Lord. May I get to know your Word better and better, and may that knowledge influence me as I approach every new decision.

If you need wisdom, ask our generous God, and he will give it to you. He will not rebuke you for asking. But when you ask him, be sure that your faith is in God alone. Do not waver. For a person with divided loyalty is as unsettled as a wave of the sea that is blown and tossed by the wind.
JAMES 1:5-6

☼ **A prayer about MEMORIES**
When I am stuck in the past

HEAVENLY FATHER,

I'm having a hard time obeying you and moving forward with your plan for my life, and I know that a big reason is because I am stuck in the past. Sometimes I hold on to memories of sinful things I used to do. Other times I hold on to regrets for mistakes I made. Either way, it's like trying to walk in two directions at once. Help me to turn away from my sinful habits and the memories that remind me of them. Teach me that when I commit to looking forward, with my eyes fixed on heaven, it will change the way I live. Keep me from looking back at what Satan offered me; that will just lead me back down the path to sin. I know that it's only by looking forward to everything you have to offer that I'll be able to overcome the memories and regrets that keep me stuck in the past. May I fix my eyes on you, Lord, and look only ahead as I follow your path for me.

The kind of sorrow God wants us to experience leads us away from sin and results in salvation. There's no regret for that kind of sorrow. 2 CORINTHIANS 7:10

☀ A prayer about GOD'S POWER
When I am amazed by the power of God

ALMIGHTY GOD,

Nothing on earth can compare to your power—not an earthquake, not a tsunami, not even the most devastating hurricane. Teach me that you can also use your power to calm the storms in my heart, dry up a flood of fear, quench the desire for sin, and control the whirlwind of my life. I'm so grateful that even though you are almighty, you still care for me.

How great is our Lord! His power is absolute! His understanding is beyond comprehension! PSALM 147:5

DAY 350 *Prayerful Moment*

☀ A prayer about CHANGE
When I'm thankful that God never changes

LORD GOD,

You are the one part of my life that never changes. I know I can always rely on you. No matter how much the circumstances of my life shift, no matter what new situations I face, you have promised to go with me, to love me, and to help me. You are my rock in a world of change.

God our Father, who created all the lights in the heavens . . . never changes or casts a shifting shadow. JAMES 1:17

☀ A prayer about CHALLENGES
When I need to take some risks

FAITHFUL LORD,

I want to be a person of great faith, and I know that people of great faith are risk takers who embrace the challenges of life. I think about examples in your Word—like Abram, who left everyone and everything he knew in response to your challenge to move to a different place. Or Moses, who had the courage to stand in front of the Red Sea with all the frightened Israelites behind him, raise his staff, and watch you make a dry path in front of him. Abram and Moses were ordinary people, but they responded in faith because they knew what you had called them to and they knew you were with them. I want to be like that, Lord! I don't want to be constantly holding back, afraid of what might happen, afraid of the challenges in front of me. I know that great things don't happen unless everyday people respond to big challenges. Embolden me with the knowledge that you are by my side. As I act boldly, in obedience, I know you will open the way for me.

Then Moses raised his hand over the sea, and the LORD opened up a path through the water with a strong east wind. The wind blew all that night, turning the seabed into dry land. So the people of Israel walked through the middle of the sea on dry ground, with walls of water on each side!
EXODUS 14:21-22

☼ A prayer about COMMITMENT
When I need to strengthen my trust in God

LORD,

Part of being committed to you means trusting you to lead me. When doubts creep in, I get distracted, wondering if you really care for me and if you will do what you say. But I keep coming back to your Word. I believe its promises, and I cling to the truth that you love me more than I can even comprehend. I know you will do what is best for me. I know you have promised all believers a glorious future with you. May my commitment allow me to trust you wholeheartedly and endure all the difficulties in my path. Even when I don't understand your ways, I can trust your heart and your love for me.

If we are faithful to the end, trusting God just as firmly as when we first believed, we will share in all that belongs to Christ. HEBREWS 3:14

☼ **A prayer about CHURCH**
When I wonder how I can contribute to my church

LORD GOD,

You have given special gifts to believers. When I look around my church, I see that some people are great organizers or administrators, while others are gifted at music, teaching, preparing food, or warmly welcoming others. I know that when everyone in a congregation uses his or her gifts to serve others, the church becomes a powerful force for good, a strong witness for you, and a mighty army to combat Satan's attacks. Help me never to doubt that I can contribute to my church. I am a part of your body—and it is not complete without me! May I find my unique place where I can effectively serve my faith community.

Just as our bodies have many parts and each part has a special function, so it is with Christ's body. We are many parts of one body, and we all belong to each other. In his grace, God has given us different gifts for doing certain things well.
ROMANS 12:4-6

☼ A prayer about COMPROMISE
When I'm not sure when to compromise

LORD,

There are lots of situations when compromising is the right thing to do—like in disagreements with friends about where to go to dinner, disagreements with classmates about the right way to approach a group project, or disagreements with a family member on how we should divide up responsibilities. But I know there are times when I should not compromise. When I'm tempted to sin, I need to say no. When others want me to compromise your truth, your ways, or your Word, I need to stand firm. Teach me that it's never right to give up godliness for something else. Give me the courage to refuse to sacrifice my morals. May my goal be to choose your ways above my own, every time, at all costs. I know that will always be a win-win situation.

You must always act in the fear of the LORD, with faithfulness and an undivided heart. 2 CHRONICLES 19:9

☼ **A prayer about PERSEVERANCE**
When I need strength to persevere

HEAVENLY FATHER,

When I'm tired and discouraged, I feel like giving up. Yet I know that will only lead to more frustration, because then my work will be unfinished. Help me to persevere through all the challenges that come my way. Give me the strength to face each setback with determination. Please teach me to keep my eyes on my end goals and trust that you are still with me, helping me. I know that persevering will help me be productive and will make my faith stronger. Please show me what you want me to learn as I persevere through difficult times.

Dear brothers and sisters, when troubles come your way, consider it an opportunity for great joy. For you know that when your faith is tested, your endurance has a chance to grow. So let it grow, for when your endurance is fully developed, you will be perfect and complete, needing nothing. JAMES 1:2-4

✾ A prayer about ANTICIPATION
When I forget about God's great plans for me

HEAVENLY FATHER,

Too often my life is filled with noise and busyness. I'm distracted by my phone or my computer, and I don't take time to be still before you. Help me to pause and wonder what momentous things you might be preparing to do next in my life. I want to come before you with reverent awe, anticipating the glorious things ahead.

"For I know the plans I have for you," says the LORD. "They are plans for good and not for disaster, to give you a future and a hope." JEREMIAH 29:11

DAY 357 *Prayerful Moment*

✾ A prayer about CONSCIENCE
When I am grateful for my conscience

MERCIFUL LORD,

I'm thankful today for the gift of my conscience. What would I do without this inner part of me that helps me know whether I am doing right or wrong, whether or not I am obeying you? Thank you for providing a way to keep me attuned to your moral guidelines. May my conscience never grow hard, Lord. May I always listen to and obey my conscience, so that I will stay sensitive to it. I want to do what is right in your sight.

Cling to your faith in Christ, and keep your conscience clear.
1 TIMOTHY 1:19

DAY 358

☼ A prayer about GOALS
When I wonder why I need goals

LORD,

I want to use my time purposefully. When I look back on my life, I want to see that I accomplished something meaningful, rather than just living on autopilot. Help me to develop goals that will keep my priorities in place. The most important things to me are maintaining my relationship with you and living in service to you, and I need to keep those two things at the forefront of my mind. I pray that my goals will motivate and energize me, giving me hope and something to live for. Through the process of setting goals, please teach me how to keep from doing too much. Remind me that you are glorified not when I stay as busy as I possibly can but when I do the things that are most important and do those to the best of my ability. Please give me vision, focus, and determination as I set and try to reach my goals.

Look straight ahead, and fix your eyes on what lies before you. Mark out a straight path for your feet; stay on the safe path. Don't get sidetracked; keep your feet from following evil.
PROVERBS 4:25-27

☼ A prayer about DESIRES
When I don't know what to do about sinful desires

LORD,

What should I do when I want things that are sinful? Sometimes I want something so strongly that I just can't think straight. Only later do I realize how selfish I was being. I become so obsessed with what I want in the moment that I forget to ask you if it's what you want for me. When I want something so strongly, help me to pause and think: Is it consistent with your Word? Is it good for me? Is it harmless to others? If the answer to any of these is no, please give me the willpower to be able to stop pursuing it. Then fill me with desires for things that do honor you—things that are right and good and beautiful and true. Those things will never harm me.

Fix your thoughts on what is true, and honorable, and right, and pure, and lovely, and admirable. Think about things that are excellent and worthy of praise. PHILIPPIANS 4:8

❄ A prayer about CONVICTIONS
When I wonder how convictions strengthen my faith

LORD JESUS,

I know that a conviction is more than just a belief; it's a commitment to a belief. It involves action, not merely empty words. May my conviction that you are who you say you are never stop at words. Instead, may it fuel my thoughts, words, and decisions. I believe you are the Son of God. I believe that you died for my sins and are my Savior. I want your teachings to permeate every aspect of my life. Strengthen my convictions, Lord Jesus. Prepare me to live out my faith and even defend it if necessary. I stake my life on you.

This will continue until we all come to such unity in our faith and knowledge of God's Son that we will be mature in the Lord, measuring up to the full and complete standard of Christ. Then we will no longer be immature like children. We won't be tossed and blown about by every wind of new teaching. We will not be influenced when people try to trick us with lies so clever they sound like the truth. Instead, we will speak the truth in love, growing in every way more and more like Christ, who is the head of his body, the church.
EPHESIANS 4:13-15

☼ A prayer about PRIDE
When I wonder how pride is affecting me

HEAVENLY FATHER,

How do I find the line between being self-confident and being proud? I know it's not your will for me to walk around gloomily, thinking everyone else in the world is more talented than I am and I have nothing to offer. That's a false view of humility. But I also know your Word tells me not to be arrogant. Teach me that pride is a problem when I start to think I am in charge and can make my own rules. It's also a problem when I think I'm more important than those around me and that my needs should somehow count more than theirs. May I never forget my true place in your Kingdom. I am your beloved child—yet I am also a sinful human being, fully dependent on you. You have given me status and security—yet I must remember that I'm not responsible for any of it. Everything I have is a gift from you. Impress that on my mind so that my pride will never get in the way of my relationship with you.

Human pride will be brought down, and human arrogance will be humbled. Only the LORD will be exalted on that day of judgment. ISAIAH 2:11

☼ A prayer about RECONCILIATION
When I need to be reconciled to someone

FATHER,

I'm so grateful that you have reconciled me to yourself. Reconciliation is at the very heart of the story of you and humankind. Ever since sin entered the world, you have been pursuing all people to reconcile them to yourself. Thank you for sending your Son to suffer on the cross so that I could be forgiven and become part of your family. Teach me, Lord, that since I've received this gift, I need to try to achieve reconciliation with others in my own life. If I'm living in unresolved conflict, my relationship with you will be harmed. Harmony in human relationships is so important that your Word even teaches me to interrupt an act of worship to first be reconciled with those around me. I pray for a humble and forgiving spirit. Give me courage to take the first step to resolve a conflict. Let me be the one to let go of my need to be right and instead extend grace. Please restore my relationships, even as my relationship with you has been beautifully restored.

If you are presenting a sacrifice at the altar in the Temple and you suddenly remember that someone has something against you, leave your sacrifice there at the altar. Go and be reconciled to that person. Then come and offer your sacrifice to God. MATTHEW 5:23-24

DAY 363 *Prayerful Moment*

✺ A prayer about TALKING TO GOD
When I need a friend

LORD,

I'm so thankful that I can talk to you about anything in my life—situations that come up at work, problems at school, challenges at home. You welcome me with open arms, whether I'm thinking deep thoughts about theology or expressing frustration about some little daily problem. May I never forget that you care for every detail of my life more than anyone in the world. Thank you for being my friend.

[Jesus said,] "I no longer call you slaves, because a master doesn't confide in his slaves. Now you are my friends." JOHN 15:15

DAY 364 *Prayerful Moment*

✺ A prayer about SALVATION
When I am humbled by your salvation

LORD JESUS,

Thank you for the wonderful gift of salvation you have offered to me freely. I have done nothing to deserve it, and I am humbled by your gift. You love me so much that you gave your life for me. You have forgiven all my sins and made me right in your sight! I don't even have words to thank you, but my heart is full of gratitude. I love you, Lord Jesus.

Since we have been made right in God's sight by faith, we have peace with God because of what Jesus Christ our Lord has done for us. ROMANS 5:1

☼ A prayer about REMEMBERING
*When I need to remember what God has done
in my life*

LORD GOD,

So many times in your Word you commanded the Israelites to remember what you had done for them—that you
had rescued them from Egypt, given them the Promised
Land, and helped them defeat the enemies who threatened
them. They needed those reminders because they were so
quick to forget and turn away from you. I know I can be
just as quick to forget. Teach me to spend time remembering how you have worked in history and in my own life.
May thinking about the past give me hope and confidence
that you will continue to help me in the future. When
I'm discouraged, encourage me to go back in my memory
to those times when I experienced your presence most
strongly. Then I will remember that you did not abandon me in the past, and you will not abandon me in the
future. You are present, working in me! May I also recount
your faithfulness before others as an act of worship and a
witness to those who need to know of your love. Thank
you that I can move toward the future with confidence,
knowing that you will be with me as you have in the past.

*We will not hide these truths from our children; we will tell
the next generation about the glorious deeds of the LORD,
about his power and his mighty wonders.* PSALM 78:4

TOPICAL INDEX